THE
RULES

THE RULES

Time-tested Secrets for Capturing the Heart of Mr. Right

BY ELLEN FEIN
AND SHERRIE SCHNEIDER

WARNER BOOKS

A Time Warner Company

Warner Books, Inc., 1271 Avenue of the Americas, New York, NY 10020

W A Time Warner Company

Printed in the United States of America

First Printing: February 1997

10 9 8 7 6 5 4 3 2

Library of Congress Cataloging-in-Publication Data

Fein, Ellen.
   The rules : time-tested secrets for capturing the heart of Mr. Right / Ellen
Fein and Sherrie Schneider.
      p.   cm
   ISBN 0-446-52291-0
   1. Dating (Social customs)   2. Mate selection—United States.
3. Men—United States—Psychology.   I. Schneider, Sherrie.
II. Title.
HQ801.F44   1995
646.7'7—dc20   94-31919
                                                                      CIP

Book design by Giorgetta Bell McRee

To our wonderful husbands
and great kids

Special thanks to
Connie Clausen

Contents

THE
RULES

Chapter I

The History of *The Rules*

*N*o one seems to remember exactly how *The Rules* got started, but we think they began circa 1917 with Melanie's grandmother who made men wait nervously in her parents' parlor in a small suburb of Michigan. Back then, they called it "playing hard to get." Whatever you call it, she had more marriage proposals than shoes. Grandma passed on her know-how to Melanie's mother, who passed it on to Melanie. It had been a family treasure for nearly a century. But when Melanie got married in 1981, she freely offered this old-fashioned advice to her single college friends and coworkers, like us.

At first, Melanie whispered *The Rules*. After all, modern women aren't to talk loudly about wanting to get married. We had grown up dreaming about being the president of the company, not the wife of the president. So, we quietly passed *The Rules* on from friend to friend, somewhat embarrassed because they seemed so, well, '50s. Still, we had to face it: as much as we loved being powerful in business, for most of us, that just wasn't enough. Like our mothers and grandmothers before us, we also wanted husbands who would be our best friends. Deep inside, if the truth be told, we really wanted to get married—the romance, the gown, the flowers, the presents, the honeymoon—the whole package. We didn't want to give up our liberation, but neither did we want to come home to empty apartments. Who said we couldn't have it all?

If you think *The Rules* are crazy, don't worry, so did we. But after much heartache we came to believe that *The Rules* aren't immoral or outlandish, just a simple working set of behaviors and reactions that, when followed, invariably serve to make most women irresistible to desirable men. Why not admit it? We needed *The Rules*! Nineties women simply have not been schooled in the basics—*The Rules* of finding a husband or at least being very popular with men.

Soon, we got bolder and began to talk louder. These *Rules*—they worked! Although they were old-fashioned and unflinching, they were extremely effective!

At first, we were uncomfortable with some of the premises which seemed to fly in the face of every-

2

thing we'd been taught about male-female relations; but—there was no getting around it—success talked. We swallowed some of our preconceived theories, followed *The Rules* faithfully, and watched as so many of us got married (along with being career women or whatever else we were).

There we were—a secret underground, sharing the magic, passing it on, doing what historically women have done for each other since the world began—networking for success. This time, though, the stakes were larger and the victories sweeter than any corporate deal. We're talking marriage here—real, lasting marriage, not just loveless mergers—the result of doing *The Rules*. The simple *Rules*. The How-to-Find-a-Swell-Husband *Rules*.

For years, we had been sharing them with the women we knew, both at home and at work. For years, women had been calling us to check up on points: "Did you say that you have to end the date first or he does? I forget."

Then one night, during a Chinese dinner in Manhattan with a few of our single friends, we heard Cindy mention something about these . . . er, *Rules* . . . that she'd heard about from a friend in California. We knew it! There could be no mistake. These were the same *Rules* one of us had followed in New York to find her wonderful husband. *The Rules* had crisscrossed the country, bouncing from woman to woman, from suburb to city, until here they came right back to us over egg rolls in Manhattan!

But—and here's the catch—Cindy got them wrong!

"*The Rule* says men have to end the date first so that they're in charge," said Cindy.

"No, no, no, WRONG. *The Rule* is *you* end the date first so that you leave him wanting you more," we explained.

It was then that we decided to write *The Rules* down so that there would be no mistakes.

What Are *The Rules?*

*H*ow many times have you heard someone say, "She's nice, she's pretty, she's smart . . . why isn't she married?" Were they talking about you, perhaps? Ever wonder why women who are not so pretty or smart attract men almost effortlessly?

Frankly, many women we know find it easier to relocate to another state, switch careers, or run a marathon than get the right man to marry them! If this sounds like you, then you need *The Rules!*

What are *The Rules?* They are a simple way of acting around men that can help any woman win the heart of the man of her dreams. Sound too good to be true? We were skeptical at first, too. Read on!

The purpose of *The Rules* is to make Mr. Right obsessed with having you as his by making yourself seem unattainable. In plain language, we're talking about playing hard to get! Follow *The Rules*, and he will not just marry you, but feel crazy about you, forever! What we're promising you is "happily ever after." A marriage truly made in heaven.

If you follow *The Rules*, you can rest assured that your husband will treat you like a queen—even when he's angry with you. Why? Because he spent so much time trying to get you. You have become so precious to him that he doesn't take you for granted. On the contrary, he thinks of you constantly. He's your best friend, your Rock of Gibraltar during bad times. He's hurt if you *don't* share your problems with him. He is always there for you—when you start your new job, if you need surgery. He even likes to get involved in mundane things, such as picking out a new bedspread. He always wants to do things *together*.

When you do *The Rules*, you don't have to worry about him chasing other women, even your very attractive neighbor or his bosomy secretary. That's because when you do *The Rules*, he somehow thinks you're the sexiest woman alive! When you do *The Rules*, you don't have to worry about being abandoned, neglected, or ignored!

A woman we know who followed *The Rules* is now married to a wonderful man who doesn't try to get rid of her to go out with the guys. Instead, he becomes slightly jealous when she does her own thing. They are very good friends, too.

Men are different from women. Women who call men, ask them out, conveniently have two tickets to a show, or offer sex on the first date destroy male ambition and animal drive. Men are born to respond to challenge. Take away challenge and their interest wanes. That, in a nutshell, is the premise of *The Rules*. Sure, a man might marry you if you don't do *The Rules*, but we can't guarantee that yours will be a good marriage.

This is how it works: if men love challenge, we become challenging! But don't ask a man if he loves challenge. He may think or even say he doesn't. He may not even realize how he reacts. *Pay attention to what he does, not what he says.*

As you read this book, you may think that *The Rules* are too calculating and wonder, "How hard to get do I have to be? Am I never to cook him dinner or take him to a Broadway show? What if I just feel like talking to him? Can't I call? When may I reveal personal things about myself?"

The answer is: Read *The Rules*. Follow them completely (not à la carte) and you will be happy you did. How many of us know women who never quite trust their husbands and always feel slightly insecure? They may even see therapists to talk about why their husbands don't pay attention to them. *The Rules* will save you about $125 an hour in therapy bills.

Of course, it's easy to do *The Rules* with men you're not that interested in. Naturally, you don't call them, instantly return their calls, or send them love letters. Sometimes your indifference makes them so crazy about you that you end up marrying one of them. That's because you did *The Rules* (without even thinking about it) and he proposed!

But settling for less is not what this book is about. The idea is to do *The Rules* with the man you're *really* crazy about. This will require effort, patience, and self-restraint. But isn't it worth it? Why should you compromise and marry someone who loves you but whom you're not crazy about? We know many women who face this dilemma. But don't worry — this book will help you marry only Mr. Right!

Your job now is to treat the man you are really, really crazy about like the man you're not that interested in — don't call, be busy sometimes! Do all of this from the beginning — from day one! Do it from the second you meet him — or should we say, the second he meets you! The better you do *The Rules* from the beginning, the harder he will fall for you.

Keep thinking, "How would I behave if I weren't that interested in him?" And then behave that way. Would you offer endless encouragement to someone you didn't really like? Would you stay on the phone with him for hours? Of course not!

Don't worry that busyness and lack of interest will drive him away. The men you don't like keep calling after you've turned them down, don't they?

Remember, *The Rules* are not about getting just any man to adore you and propose; they're about getting the man of your dreams to marry you! It's an old-fashioned formula, but it really works!

We understand why modern, career-oriented women have sometimes scoffed at our suggestions. They've been MBA-trained to "make things happen" and to take charge of their careers. However, a relationship with a man is different from a job. In a relationship, the man must take charge. He must propose. We are not making this up—biologically, he's the aggressor.

Some women complain that *The Rules* prevent them from being themselves or having fun. "Why should dating be work?" some ask. But when they end up alone on Saturday night because they did not follow *The Rules*, they always come back to us saying, "Okay, okay, tell me what to do."

Doing what you want to do is not always in your best interest. On a job interview, you don't act "like yourself." You don't eat cake if you're serious about losing weight. Similarly, it is not wise to let it all hang out and break *The Rules* as soon as you begin dating a man.

In the long run, it's not fun to break *The Rules*! You could easily end up alone. Think long term. Imagine a husband you love, beautiful sex, children, companionship, and growing old with someone who thinks you're a great catch.

Think about never having to be alone on Saturday nights or having to ask your married friends to fix you up. Think about being a couple! Unfortunately, however, you must experience some delayed gratification in the first few months of the relationship to achieve this marital bliss. But has wearing your heart on your sleeve ever gotten you anywhere?

There are many books and theories on this subject. All make wonderful promises, but *The Rules* actually produce results. It's easy to know what's going on when you do *The Rules*. It's very simple. If he calls you, pursues you, asks you out, it's *The Rules*. If you have to make excuses for his behavior—for example, he didn't call after the first date because he's still hung up on his ex-girlfriend—and you have to think about every word he said until your head hurts and you call him, it's not *The Rules*. Forget what he's going through—for example, "fear of commitment" or "not ready for a relationship." Remember, we don't play therapist when we do *The Rules*. If he calls and asks you out, it's *The Rules*. Anything else is conversation.

Chapter III

Meet a *Rules* Girl

*I*f you had ever met Melanie, you wouldn't have thought she was extraordinarily pretty or smart or special, but you might have noticed that she had a way of behaving around men that put prom queens to shame. Melanie did the best with what she had: she wore makeup and clothes well, and acted elusive. Unlike other, prettier girls who ran after men or made themselves available every time a man called, Melanie acted indifferent—sometimes aloof, sometimes nice, but always *happy and busy*. She didn't return their calls, didn't stare at them (a dead giveaway of interest, see *Rule #3*), and always ended phone conversations first. "I've got a million things to do" was her favorite closing line. Melanie's boyfriend eventually proposed to the one girl he thought he would never get—her!

Who hasn't met a Melanie? Haven't we all known women who seemed to be experts around men? Men don't appear to unnerve these women or trip them up. They have a certain self-confidence around men that has nothing to do with their looks or their jobs. Melanies simply feel *good* about themselves—they can take or leave men—which makes men have to have them. Call it reverse psychology or whatever you want, but Melanies always get their man.

When you meet a Melanie, especially a plain and simple Melanie, you want to go up to her and ask, "What is it, what are you doing that make men run after you? What's your secret? What am *I* doing wrong?" A genuine Melanie would probably say without too much thought, "Oh, it's really nothing." The born-again Melanies—former *Rules* breakers who have learned their lesson after being burned by chasing men—would probably say, "Yes, there is a secret. Men love a challenge. Don't talk to them first, be busy sometimes, turn them down once in a while (nicely!)."

You will find Melanies everywhere you go. Watch them carefully. Observe how they have made self-contentment and independence an art form. They don't look wildly around to catch men's eyes. They don't say hello first. They just go about their business.

It would probably be good practice the next time you are at a social event to stand back and watch the Melanies and *The Rules* breakers. Compare how the two types of women behave around men and notice the results. Notice how the Melanies intentionally don't carry a pen with them in order to give men their phone numbers and they don't rush to give their business cards. Notice the way they move around the room while *The Rules* breakers stand too long in one place, look anxious, or talk too long to one man. They make it too easy for men to ask them out—and, as you will read in this book, that's a big mistake.

One day, after years of watching girls like Melanie snag the men of our dreams, we asked Melanie how she got such a great catch. She took pity on us and told us about *The Rules*. She said that we were nice but we talked too much and were overly eager, and that we mistakenly tried to be "friends" with men rather than elusive butterflies, or, as she put it, "creatures unlike any other" (see *Rule #1*).

Needless to say, we were offended by what seemed to us to be downright trickery and manipulation. *The Rules* would send women back twenty-five years. What would the feminists say? On the other hand, Melanie had what *we* wanted: the husband of her dreams who adored her. It made sense to rethink our offended psyches!

Melanie assured us that plain-looking women who followed *The Rules* stood a better chance of being happily married than gorgeous women who didn't. Thinking back on our own dating history, it did appear that the men we really wanted didn't necessarily

13

want us. We'd be ourselves, friendly and supportive, and they thought we were great—but it ended right there. And, come to think of it, the ones we didn't particularly care for, the ones we didn't notice, maybe even snubbed, were the ones who didn't stop calling, the ones who were crazy about us. There was a message here somewhere: treat the men we *wanted* like the men we *didn't* want.

Simple, but not easy. But what did we have to lose? We wanted what Melanie had. So we did what she did, and—it worked!

Chapter IV——————————————————

But First the Product—You!

*B*efore *The Rules* can be applied for the best, most unbelievable results—the man of your dreams asking you to marry him—you have to be the best you can be. Certainly not perfect or gorgeous, but the best you can be, so . . .

Look your best! The better you look, the better you will feel, and the more desirable you will become to him. Maybe other men will start finding you more attractive and asking you out. You will no longer feel that the man you're currently dating is the only man on earth. You'll be less anxious and more confident. And when you look and feel good, you're less likely to break *The Rules*.

We are not nutritionists, but we do know that eating right—protein, fruits, and vegetables—makes you feel good. And that exercise releases endorphins which make you feel happier and more energetic. So, in addition to a healthy diet, we strongly suggest that you shake your buns! Join a gym, buy an exercise video, or go jogging in a nearby park(also a great place to meet men who are jogging or walking their dogs). Make exercise exciting by playing music while you do sit-ups.

Diet and exercise and *The Rules* have a lot in common. Both require putting long-term goals before short-term gratification. You will have to experience a certain amount of discomfort when you can't eat a cookie and you can't call a man. But you want to be fit and you want to get married, so you do what you have to do. Make friends with a woman in the same predicament and jog together, go to dances together, and reprimand each other when either of you is tempted to break *The Rules*. You don't have to do all this hard work alone!

If you are serious about finding a husband, then you must change your definition of gratification. Gratification is a man calling you, pursuing you, and asking you to marry him. Gratification is *not* a hot fudge sundae or a hot date where you break *The Rules!*

Self-improvement will help you catch and keep a man. So try to change bad habits like slovenliness if you expect to live with a man. Men like women who are neat and clean. They also make better mothers of their children—the kind who don't lose their kids at the beach.

Now a word about clothes. If you walk around in any old clothes on the theory that what counts is only what's inside, not your outside, think again! Men like women who wear fashionable, sexy clothes in bright colors. Why not please them?

If you don't know a lot about clothes, read fashion magazines like *Cosmopolitan, Vogue, Glamour,* and *Mirabella* and books on the subject; consult a friend whose taste you admire; or enlist the help of a personal shopper at a department store. Trying on clothes by yourself in a dressing room can be overwhelming and confusing—not to mention painful if you are out of shape—so it's always good to get a second opinion. Why not a professional one? Personal shoppers can help you find clothes that look good on you and that hide your flaws, as opposed to clothes that are perhaps trendy but not flattering.

Always remember when you are shopping that you are unique, a creature unlike any other, a woman. Don't aspire to the unisex look. Buy feminine-looking clothes to wear on the weekends as well as during the workweek. Remember that you're dressing for men, not other women, so always strive to look feminine.

While it's good to keep up with the times, don't be a fashion slave. Don't spend a month's salary, say, on bell bottoms and clogs just because they happen to be in vogue this year. First of all, they may not be around next season, and, more importantly, you may not look good in them! We know women who have gone overboard with one look—be it man-tailored suits or oversized crocheted sweaters—and ended up looking overdressed, trendy, and not at all sexy. Be a smart shopper, not a runaway spender! Buy a few good classics and mix them with cheaper items.

Keep in mind that just because something is in vogue doesn't mean that it will look good on you or appeal to men. Men don't necessarily care for the "waif" look or like it when women wear long granny dresses and combat boots, however popular the look may be. They like women in feminine clothes. Wear a short skirt (but not too short), if you have the legs for it.

Also, don't feel that you have to wear designer clothes to attract men. Men don't care whose label you're wearing, just how your clothes look and fit on you. It's better to buy a no-name brand that looks stunning and hides your hips than a designer outfit that doesn't.

While you're shopping in a department store, stop by a cosmetics counter and treat yourself to a makeover. We can all look better than we do. Many of us don't realize our potential until we get a makeover, which, by the way, is often given for free with a minimal purchase. Pay attention to which colors are good for you and how the makeup artist applies them. Buy whatever he or she suggests that you can afford and go home and practice putting it on.

Don't leave the house without wearing makeup. Put lipstick on even when you go jogging!

Do everything you possibly can to put your best face forward. If you have a bad nose, get a nose job; color gray hair; grow your hair long. Men prefer long hair, something to play with and caress. It doesn't matter what your hairdresser and friends think. You're certainly not trying to attract them! Let's face it, hairdressers are notorious for pushing exciting, short haircuts on their clients; trimming long hair is not fun for them. It doesn't matter that short hair is easier to wash and dry or that your hair is very thin. The point is, we're girls! We don't want to look like boys.

It will be easier to feel like a creature unlike any other if you follow good grooming. Manicures, pedicures, periodic facials, and massages should become part of your routine. And don't forget to spray on an intoxicating perfume when you go out—just don't overdo it.

Now that you look the part, you must act the part. Men like women. Don't act like a man, even if you are head of your own company. Let him open the door. Be feminine. Don't tell sarcastic jokes. Don't be a loud, knee-slapping, hysterically funny girl. This is okay when you're alone with your girlfriends. But when you're with a man you like, be quiet and mysterious, act ladylike, cross your legs and smile. Don't talk so much. Wear black sheer pantyhose and hike up your skirt to entice the opposite sex! You might feel offended by these suggestions and argue that this will suppress your intelligence or vivacious personality. You may feel that you won't be able to be yourself, but men will love it!

In addition, don't sound cynical or depressed and tell long-winded stories of all the people who have hurt you or let you down. Don't make your prospective husband a savior or therapist. On the contrary, act as if you were born happy. Don't tell everything about yourself. Say thank you and please. Practice this ladylike behavior with waiters, doormen, and even cab drivers who take the long way to your destination. This will make it easier to be ladylike on dates.

If you never meet men accidentally, go to everything—dances, tennis parties (even if you don't play tennis), Club Med. Just go, go, go—show up! Put a personal ad in a magazine, answer ads, ask people to set you up. Don't shy away from singles events with the rationalization that "The men who go there aren't my type." Remember, you are not trying to find large groups of men who are your type, just one! Don't lose sight of this concept. It will keep you going on those bad days when you are convinced that true love is just never going to happen to you!

Last but not least, trust this process. You may not meet your husband immediately after you have gotten in shape, bought some terrific outfits, and practiced *The Rules* on three eligible men. It may not be your time. But it is our experience that if you continue to do *The Rules* at every opportunity and pray for patience, you will eventually meet and marry the man of your dreams.

Rule #1

Be a "Creature Unlike Any Other"

*B*eing a creature unlike any other is a state of mind. You don't have to be rich, beautiful, or exceptionally smart to feel this way about yourself. And you don't have to be born with this feeling either. It can be learned, practiced, and mastered, like all the other rules in this book.

Being a creature unlike any other is really an attitude, a sense of confidence and radiance that permeates your being from head to toe. It's the way you smile (you light up the room), pause in between sentences (you don't babble on and on out of nervousness), listen (attentively), look (demurely, never stare), breathe (slowly), stand (straight), and walk (briskly, with your shoulders back).

It doesn't matter if you're not a beauty queen, that

you never finished college, or that you don't keep up with current events. You still think you're enough! You have more confidence than women with MBAs or money in the bank. You don't grovel. You're not desperate or anxious. You don't date men who don't want you. You trust in the abundance and goodness of the universe: if not him, someone better, you say. You don't settle. You don't chase anyone. You don't use sex to make men love you. You believe in love and marriage. You're not cynical. You don't go to pieces when a relationship doesn't work out. Instead, you get a manicure and go out on another date or to a singles dance. You're an optimist. You brush away a tear so that it doesn't smudge your makeup and you move on! Of course, that is not how you really *feel.* This is how you *pretend* you feel until it feels real. *You act as if!*

On a date, you never show that getting married is foremost on your mind. You're cool. He may think you've turned down several marriage proposals. You sip—never slurp—your drink and let him find out all about you, instead of the other way around. Your answers are short, light, and flirtatious. Your gestures are soft and feminine. When your hair falls in front of your face, you tilt your head back and comb back your hair with your hand from the top of your head in a slow, sweeping motion.

All your movements—the way you excuse yourself to use the ladies room or look at your watch to end the date—are fluid and sexy, not jerky or self-conscious. You've been on many dates before; you're a pro. That's because you take care of yourself. You didn't lie in bed depressed, eating cookies before the date. You took a bubble bath, read this book, and built up your soul with positive slogans like, "I'm a beautiful woman. I am enough." You told yourself that you don't have to do anything more on the date than show up. He'll either love you or not. It's not your fault if he doesn't call again. You're beautiful, inside and out. Someone else will love you if he doesn't. All that matters is that you end the date first (see *Rule #11*).

When you go to singles dances or parties, you pump yourself up. You pretend you're a movie star. You hold your head high and walk in as if you just flew in from Paris on the Concorde. You're only in town for one night and if some lucky hunk doesn't swoop down and grab you it'll be his loss!

You get a drink, a Perrier perhaps, even if you're not thirsty. It keeps your hands busy so you don't bite your nails or twirl your hair out of nervousness. You don't show that you're nervous, even if you are. That's the secret: you act as if everything's great, even if you're on the verge of flunking college or getting fired. You walk briskly, as if you know where you're going, which is just around the room. You keep moving. You don't stand in a corner waiting for anyone. They have to catch you in motion.

If you think you aren't pretty, if you think other girls are better dressed or thinner or cooler, you keep it to yourself. You tell yourself, "Any man would be lucky to have me," until it sinks in and you start to believe it. If a man approaches you, you smile and answer his questions very nicely without saying too much. You're demure, a bit mysterious. You leave him hungry for more, as opposed to bored. After a few minutes you say, "I think I'll walk around now."

Most women hang around men all night waiting to be asked to dance. But you do *The Rules*. If he wants to be with you or get your phone number, he'll search the crowded room until he finds you. You don't offer him *your* pen or business card. You don't make it easy for him. Don't even carry them with you or you may be tempted to "help him out." The reason is that *he* has to do all the work. As he scrambles around begging the coat-check girl for a pen, you stand by quietly. You think to yourself, "*The Rules* have begun!"

It's that simple. You do *The Rules* and trust that one day a prince will notice that you're different from all other women he's known, and ask for your hand!

Don't Talk to a Man First (and Don't Ask Him to Dance)

*N*ever? Not even "Let's have coffee" or "Do you come here often?" Right, not even these seemingly harmless openers. Otherwise, how will you know if he spotted you first, was smitten by you and had to have you, or is just being polite?

We know what you're thinking. We know how extreme such a rule must sound, not to mention snobbish, silly, and painful; but taken in the context of *The Rules*, it makes perfect sense. After all, the premise of *The Rules* is that we never make anything happen, that we trust in the natural order of things — namely, that man pursues woman.

By talking to a man first, we interfere with whatever was supposed to happen or not happen, perhaps causing a conversation or a date to occur that was never meant to be and inevitably getting hurt in the process. Eventually, he'll talk to the girl he really wants and drop you.

Yet, we manage to rationalize this behavior by telling ourselves, "He's shy" or "I'm just being friendly." Are men really shy? We might as well tackle this question right now. Perhaps a therapist would say so, but we believe that most men are not shy, just not *really, really* interested if they don't approach you. It's hard to accept that, we know. It's also hard waiting for the right one—the one who talks to you first, calls, and basically does most of the work in the beginning of the relationship because he must have you.

It's easy to rationalize women's aggressive behavior in this day and age. Unlike years ago when women met men at dances and "coming out" parties and simply waited for one to pick them out of the crowd and start a conversation, today many women are accountants, doctors, lawyers, dentists, and in management positions. They work with men, for men, and men work for them. Men are their patients and their clients. How can a woman not talk to a man first?

The Rules answer is to treat men you are interested in like any other client or patient or coworker, as hard as that may be. Let's face it, when a woman meets a man she really likes, a lightbulb goes on in her head and she sometimes, without realizing it, re-laxes, laughs, and spends more time with him than is necessary. She may suggest lunch to discuss something that could be discussed over the phone because she is hoping to ignite some romance. This is a common ploy. Some of the smartest women try to make things happen under the guise of business. They think they are too educated or talented to be passive, play games, or do *The Rules*. They feel their diplomas and paychecks entitle them to do more in life than wait for the phone to ring. These women, we assure you, always end up heartbroken when their forward-ness is rebuffed. But why shouldn't it be? Men know what they want. No one has to ask *them* to lunch.

So, the short of it is that if you meet men profes-sionally, you still have to do *The Rules*. You must wait until he brings up lunch or anything else beyond business. As we explain in *Rule #17*, the man must take the lead. Even if you are making the same amount of money as a man you are interested in, he must bring up lunch. If you refuse to accept that men and women are different romantically, even though they may be equal professionally, you will behave like men—talk to them first, ask for their phone number, invite them to discuss the case over dinner at your place—and drive them away. Such forward-ness is very risky; sometimes we have seen it work, most of the time it doesn't and it *always* puts the woman through hell emotionally. By not accepting the concept that the man must pursue the woman, women put themselves in jeopardy of being rejected or ignored, if not at the moment, then at some point in the future. We hope you never have to endure the following torture:

Our dentist friend Pam initiated a friendship with Robert when they met in dental school several years ago by asking him out to lunch. *She spoke to him first.* Although they later became lovers and even lived together, he never seemed really "in love" with her and her insecurity about the relationship never went away. Why would it? *She spoke to him first.* He recently broke up with her over something trivial. The truth is he never loved her. Had Pam followed *The Rules*, she would never have spoken to Robert or initiated anything in the first place. Had she followed *The Rules*, she might have met someone else who truly wanted her. She would not have wasted time. *Rules* girls don't waste time.

Here's another example of a smart woman who broke *The Rules:* Claudia, a confident Wall Street broker, spotted her future husband on the dance floor of a popular disco and planted herself next to him for a good five minutes. When he failed to make the first move, she told herself that he was probably shy or had two left feet and asked him to dance. The relationship has been filled with problems. She often complains that he's as "shy" in the bedroom as he was that night on the dance floor.

A word about dances. It's become quite popular these days for women to ask men to dance. Lest there is any doubt in your mind, this behavior is totally against *The Rules*. If a man doesn't bother to walk across the room to seek you out and ask you to dance, then he's obviously not interested and asking him to dance won't change his feelings or rather his lack of feelings for you. He'll probably be flattered that you asked and dance with you just to be polite and he might even want to have sex with you that night, but he won't be crazy about you. Either he didn't notice you or you made it too easy. He never got the chance to pursue you and this fact will always permeate the relationship even if he does ask you out.

We know what you're thinking: what am I supposed to do all night if no one asks me to dance? Unfortunately, the answer is to go to the bathroom five times if you have to, reapply your lipstick, powder your nose, order more water from the bar, think happy thoughts, walk around the room in circles until someone notices you, make phone calls from the lobby to your married friends for encouragement—in short, anything but ask a man to dance. Dances are not necessarily fun for us. They may be fun for other women who just want to go out and have a good time. But you're looking for love and marriage so you can't always do what you feel like. You have to do *The Rules*. That means that even when you're bored or lonely, you don't ask men to dance. Don't even stand next to someone you like, hoping he'll ask you, as many women do. You have to *wait* for someone to notice you. You might have to go home without having met anyone you liked or even danced one dance. But tell yourself that at least you got to practice *The Rules* and there's always another dance. You walk out with a sense of accomplishment that at least you didn't break *The Rules!*

If this sounds boring, remember the alternative is worse. Our good friend Sally got so resentful of having to dance with all the "losers" at a particular party that she finally decided to defy *The Rules* she knew only too well and asked the best-looking man in the room to dance. Not only was he flattered, but they danced for hours and he asked her out for the next three nights. "Maybe there are exceptions to *The Rules*," she thought triumphantly. She found out otherwise, of course. It seems Mr. Right was in town for just a few days on business and had a girlfriend on the West Coast. No wonder he hadn't asked anyone to dance that night. He probably just went to the party to have fun, not to find his future wife. The moral of the story: don't figure out why someone hasn't asked you to dance—there's always a good reason.

Unfortunately, more women than men go to dances to meet "The One." Their eagerness and anxiety get the best of them and they end up talking to men first or asking them to dance. So you must condition yourself not to expect anything from a dance. View it simply as an excuse to put on high heels, apply a new shade of blush, and be around a lot of people. Chances are someone of the opposite sex will start to talk to *you* at some point in the evening. If and when he does, and you're not having such a great time, don't show it. For example, don't be clever or cynical and say, "I would have been better off staying home and watching *Seinfeld*." Men aren't interested in women who are witty in a negative way. If someone asks if you're having a good time, simply say yes and smile.

If you find all of this much too hard to do, then don't go to the dance. Stay home, do sit-ups, watch *Seinfeld*, and reread *The Rules*. It's better to stay home and read *The Rules* than go out and break them.

Don't Stare at Men or Talk Too Much

*L*ooking at someone first is a dead giveaway of interest. Let him look at *you!* If he doesn't notice you first, he's probably not interested. Keep walking, someone else will notice you.

Did you know that there are workshops designed to teach women how to make eye contact with men they find attractive? Save your money. It is never necessary to make eye contact. What about letting men know you're receptive? We suggest simply smiling at the room (or the universe, if you will), and looking relaxed and approachable. That's how to acknowledge a man's attention, not by staring at him. Don't look anxiously around for "The One." That is certain to make anyone look the other way. There is nothing attractive about anxiety.

On the first date, avoid staring romantically into his eyes. Otherwise, he will know that you're planning the honeymoon. Instead, look down at the table or your food, or simply survey the crowd at the restaurant. It's best to seem generally interested in life, in others, in your surroundings, in the paintings on the wall, as opposed to this live prey. He will feel crowded and self-conscious if you gaze at him too much. Restrain yourself. Let him spend the evening trying to get *your* attention.

One of the hardest aspects of dating is figuring out what to say. Do you talk about the weather or politics? Should you be intellectual or girlish? If you're smart, you'll stay cool and just listen to what he says. Follow his lead. If he wants to talk about dance clubs, tell him which ones you've been to and which ones you like. We're not suggesting that you be an airhead. On the contrary! It's just that you're easy to be with. When appropriate, show him that you keep up with current events and have interests.

Early dating is *not* the time to tell him about your job problems. In general, don't be too heavy. But don't be funny if he's serious. Just go with the flow.

Needless to say, there will be moments on a date when neither of you has anything to say. Don't feel the need to fill in these silences. You'll end up saying something stupid and forced. Sometimes men just want to drive in silence without saying a word. Let them. Maybe he's thinking about how he's going to propose to you one day. Don't ruin his concentration.

Don't feel you have to be entertaining or have interesting conversation all the time. He will think you are trying too hard. Just be there! Remember, men fall in love with your essence, not with anything in particular you say.

If anything, men should be the ones scrambling their brains to come up with clever lines, asking you a lot of questions, and wondering whether or not they're keeping you interested. Besides, most men find chatty women annoying. We know one man who stopped calling a woman he was physically attracted to because she simply didn't stop talking. Don't be like that. As a woman, you probably like to talk, *especially* about the relationship, but you must hold your tongue. Wait until the date is over and then you can call ten girlfriends and analyze the date for hours.

On the date itself, be quiet and reserved. He'll wonder what you're thinking, if you like him, and if he's making a good impression. He'll think you're interesting and mysterious, unlike many of the women he's dated. Don't you want him to think about you like that?

Don't Meet Him Halfway or Go Dutch on a Date

*M*en love a challenge—that's why they play sports, fight wars, and raid corporations. The worst thing you can do is make it easy for them. When a man is trying to set up a date to meet you, don't say, "Actually, I'm going to be in your area anyway"; don't offer the names of restaurants between your place and his, unless he asks. Don't say much at all. Let him do all the thinking, the talking, let him flip through the Yellow Pages or magazine listings and call a couple of friends for suggestions to come up with a place convenient for you. Men really feel good when they work hard to see you. Don't take that away from them.

The Rule is that men are supposed to rearrange their schedules around you, pursue you, take cabs and trains to see you. For example, on their second date, Charles drove forty miles out of his way to see Darlene because she was spending the weekend at her mother's. Most girls would have left their moms in the lurch so that their date wouldn't have to be inconvenienced. But Darlene was schooled in *The Rules* and knew the right thing to do. The extra miles only made Charles more determined to see her.

Friends and colleagues meet halfway. Men (real men) pick up women at their apartments or offices for dates. Always make the place convenient for you. We don't care where you live.

Invariably, we find that men who insist that their dates meet them halfway or (worse) on their own turf, turn out to be turds—inconsiderate, uncompromising, and even miserly. Jane recalls that after cabbing from Greenwich Village to Brooklyn Heights to meet Steve (a blind date) at his favorite brunch place, he suggested they split the check.

Jane, a truly nice person, agreed that it was only fair to pay her share. After all, she made a considerable amount of money as a lawyer and felt it would be "unfair" for Steve to "absorb" the entire cost of the date. Why should he have to pick up the whole tab? That was very nice of Jane, but we assure you that had she insisted that they meet at a place near her, perhaps just for a drink (especially if she didn't feel right spending his money), Steve would have treated her like a princess, not a coworker. But since

Jane made everything so easy for him, he didn't treat her well, lost interest, and eventually stopped calling.

It's not that women aren't capable of taking subways and paying for themselves. It's just chivalrous, hence *The Rules*, for men to pick up their dates and pick up the checks. Equality and Dutch treat are fine in the workplace, but not in the romantic playing field. Love is *easy* when the man pursues the woman and pays for the woman most of the time. He feels that the money he spends on the food, the movie, and the cabs is the price of being with you and it's worth every penny. You should feel honored, happy, not guilty.

But if part of you feels uncomfortable about him paying for everything, offer to leave the tip or, if the night is a long one—say, dinner, a show, and three cab rides or parking—pay for something small along the way. But don't pay for anything on the first three dates. Later on, you can reciprocate in your own way: cook him dinner at your place or buy him a baseball cap. If he's on a tight budget or is a student and you're worried about him spending tuition money, still don't split the check. Instead, suggest inexpensive places to eat and have a hamburger. Don't order appetizers or more than one drink. There's always pizza or Chinese food. Suggest movies, museums, and cheap outdoor concerts, not Broadway plays.

It's nice of you to care about his finances, but remember that he is deriving great pleasure from taking you out. Why deprive him of the joy of feeling chivalrous? Actually, the best way you can repay him is by being appreciative. Say thank you and please. Don't criticize the place or the food or the service, even if they are plain awful. Be positive. Look for the good in everything. We know one man who became even more enamored of a girl on their second date because she didn't complain one word when he couldn't remember where he parked at a football game. For the whole hour during which they pounded the pavement looking for his car, he kept thinking, "What a great girl!"

Many things can go wrong on a date, especially when a guy is so eager to impress you that he ends up making more mistakes—locking his keys in the car, forgetting the theater tickets, and so on. Never use these blunders to make him feel bad. Instead, see all the effort and expense he is putting into the date. Being a good sport could make the difference between being just another date and his future wife.

Don't Call Him and Rarely Return His Calls

*I*f you are following *The Rules* religiously, there is no reason to call him. He should be calling you, and calling you again and again until he pins you down for a date.

To call men is to pursue them, which is totally against *The Rules*. They will immediately know that you like them and possibly lose interest! Another reason not to call men is so you don't catch them in the middle of something—watching a football game, paying bills, entertaining a friend, or even sleeping— when they may not be in the mood to talk to you. Why take a chance?

Invariably, when *you* call him, he will get off the phone first or quickly and you might misinterpret his busyness as disinterest. *You* may even think that he's with another woman! Understandably, you feel empty and nervous for the rest of the day or evening or until you hear from him again. This nervousness might make you call him *again* to ask, "Is everything okay?" or "Do you still love me? miss me?" And, you end up breaking more rules!

So, if you don't want a man to know how much you like him, or that you feel empty and insecure, don't call him. If he leaves a message on your machine to return his call, try not to. Only call him back right away if it's a scheduling change regarding an upcoming date or event, not just to chat.

Not calling will leave him desiring you more, make him want to see you again and call you again. It prevents him from getting to know all about you much too quickly and getting bored. Besides, when you call only once in a while, it becomes special.

Don't worry about seeming rude. When he loves you or wants to get in touch with you badly, he won't think you're rude, just busy or hard to get—and men always call again.

Have you ever noticed that the conversation is always better when men call you? That's because when they call you, they're doing the dialing, they want you, miss you at that moment, and can't wait to hear your voice. When they call you, they're the aggressor, they've thought about what they're going to say and have made the time to say it. They're available!

The Rules work for you when they call you because

you may not be home and they'll wonder where you are or have to call again. When they call you, you might be busy and have to nicely cut the conversation short. It will be easier to do *Rule #6: Always End Phone Calls First*, when you let them call you.

But none of us are saints, and the reality is that we sometimes have to call men back. Not call them, mind you, just call them back. If, for whatever reason, you have to return a man's calls, try to wait. Don't call right back. When you do, keep the conversation short and sweet. Don't tell his machine what time and what nights you can be reached or volunteer any additional information about how he can reach you. That would be making it too easy for him and you will appear too eager. Let him figure it out! Remember, you're a *Rules* girl and you're very busy! A *Rules* girl typically comes home to many messages on her answering machine from men trying to fill up her weekends.

Now what if he leaves a message on your machine on Tuesday night and you're dying to get a Saturday night date out of him? Do you call back Tuesday night? *The Rules* answer is no because it will seem obvious that you are probably calling to get a Saturday night date. Better that *he* call *you* again by Wednesday night (the absolute cutoff) for a Saturday night date. Better not to have a date on Saturday night than to get in the habit of calling him. *The Rules* are not about getting a date, but a husband. Don't win the battle and lose the war.

Remember, *The Rules* are also about not getting hurt or dumped. We never want you to go through unnecessary pain. Life has enough pain without our adding man pain to it. We can't control cancer or drunk drivers, but we can restrain ourselves from dialing his number. If you call him and he doesn't return your call or doesn't ask you out, you'll be crushed. If you call him, he'll think you're not so elusive and he won't have to work so hard. If you call him, he won't get trained to ask you out at the end of each date. He has to learn that if he doesn't ask you out when he sees you, he might not reach you on the phone so soon and not see you for a week or two. It's not that you're *impossible* to get, you're just *hard* to get. Remember, you're very busy with activities and other dates and you make plans ahead of time. But don't reprimand him for not calling sooner by saying, "If you had called earlier . . ." Just say, "Really, I'd love to, but I can't." (He'll figure out he has to call sooner.)

If he's in love with you, he'll start calling Monday or Tuesday for Saturday night. If he doesn't love you, then he won't call you again and again until he pins you down.

However, don't be surprised if a man takes a week or two after the first date to call. He may have a lot of things going on, or he may be dating other women. He may be trying to fit you into his schedule but just isn't sure how to do it. Remember, he had a life before he met you! Don't flip out! Just get busy (so you don't think about him twenty-four hours a day). Give him space, wait for *him* to call.

Here's a good example of how to handle such a situation: Our friend Laura waited two and a half weeks after her first date with David to hear from him. David was newly divorced and needed time to think before jumping into another relationship. A *Rules* girl, Laura gave him time and space. Unlike most women, she didn't call to "see how he was doing" or with some other excuse like, "Didn't you say you needed the name of my financial planner?" Sure, Laura was hurt, but she made plans with friends and went on blind dates. She had a pragmatic attitude. She knew that if he liked her, he'd eventually call; if he didn't, it was his loss! *Next!* When David finally called, she was nice and friendly. She didn't demand to know why he didn't call sooner and want to *talk* about it. They dated for ten months and are married now.

One last thought about the phone: sometimes we want to call a man we are dating not to speak to him, but just to hear his voice. We feel that we are simply going to die if we don't hear his sexy voice this minute! That's understandable. We suggest you call his home answering machine when he's at work. Hang up before the beep. It really works!

Always End Phone Calls First

*D*on't call men (see *Rule #5*), except to occasionally return their calls. When a man calls you, don't stay on the phone for more than ten minutes. Buy a timer if you have to. When the bell rings, you have to go! That way you seem busy and you won't give away too much about yourself or your plans (even if you don't have any plans). By ending the conversation first, you leave them wanting more. Good conversation enders are: "I have a million things to do," "Well, it's been really nice talking to you," "Actually, I'm kinda busy right now," and "My beeper's beeping, gotta run!" Remember to say these things in a very nice way.

Women love to talk. And one of their biggest faults is talking to men as if they were their girlfriends, therapists, or next-door neighbors. Remember, early on in a relationship, the man is the adversary (if he's someone you really like). He has the power to hurt you by never calling again, by treating you badly, or by being around but indifferent. While it's also true that you can reject him, the fact is that it's the man who notices you, asks you out, and ultimately proposes marriage. He runs the show. The best way to protect yourself from pain is to not get emotionally involved too quickly.

So don't stay on the phone for an hour or two recounting your feelings or every incident of the day. You'll become transparent very quickly and run the risk of making him tired or bored. He does not want to date his crazy younger sister, his chatterbox mother, or his gossipy next-door neighbor. He wants to talk to a girl who's friendly, light, and breezy. By getting off the phone first, you don't have to wonder if you've kept him on too long, bored him, or revealed too much about yourself. Because it can be very difficult to monitor the amount of time you spend on the phone when you are "in like" or in love, we again suggest using a timer or stopwatch. When the bell rings, you sweetly say, "I really have to go now." A timer is objective; you are not.

It doesn't matter if you're having a great conversation and you want to tell him all about what happened to you between the ages of five and six that shaped your life. When the bell rings, the conversation is over. Remember, you always want to be mysterious. Having to get off the phone first creates a certain amount of mystery in his mind. He'll wonder why you have to go so soon, what you're doing, and if you're dating someone else. It's good for him to wonder about you. *The Rules* (and a timer) will make him wonder about you a lot.

You may think that men will find your abruptly ending a phone call rude and won't call again. On the contrary, just the opposite often happens simply because men are irrational when it comes to love. For example, our friend Cindy set her timer to four minutes one evening. "Gotta go," she said at the sound of the bell. Five minutes later he called back to insist that they start seeing each other twice a week instead of once a week. The four-minute call worked like a charm, bringing him closer to her, not (as you would expect) farther away.

If you're a genuinely nice person, you will probably feel cruel when you do *The Rules*. You will think you are making men suffer, but in reality you are actually doing them a favor. By doing *The Rules*, you make men want to spend more time with you on the phone and in person. They get to experience longing! Tell yourself you are doing them a favor when you feel heartless about doing *The Rules*!

Another tip for driving a man to madness is to turn off your answering machine on a Sunday afternoon, and see if he doesn't go crazy trying to pin you down. When Cindy tried this tactic, her boyfriend ended up calling so many times that day that he activated her answering machine. (Some machines will automatically turn on after fourteen rings. Can you imagine him letting it ring fourteen times?!) When he finally got her on the phone that night, he possessively asked, "Where have you been? I wanted to take you for a drive in the country." It's good when men get upset; it means they care about you. If they're not angry, they're indifferent, and if they're indifferent, they've got one foot out the door. Getting off the phone after a few minutes is not easy, but it works.

Our friend Jody felt that she was "losing" Jeff, her boyfriend of three months, when after a Saturday night date he said good-bye very casually and told her, "I'll call ya. I'll let you know what's a good night for *me* next week." Jody felt the tables turning and took an extreme but necessary *Rules* action. She didn't answer her phone the night he usually called. She just listened to it ring and ring. When he finally reached her the next day at work, he was a little less cocky and somewhat nervous. He asked her what night would be good for *her*! The phone strategy worked — he never pulled another stunt like that again.

Here's another phone tip: if you're home on a Friday night because you're tired or don't have a date, leave the answering machine on or have your mom or roommate say you're not home. That way, if by some chance he calls you on a Friday night because he's not doing anything either, he'll think you're not home. The worst thing you can do is give him the impression that you aren't busy and sought after by other men. Don't let him think that you're a couch potato, even if you are. Don't think playing games is bad. Sometimes game playing is good. Men like to think that they are getting the prom queen. Show him that you have a full life, that you are independent.

On any other night when he calls and you pick up the phone, don't feel you have to tell him exactly what you are doing. After a few minutes, just say you're busy (nicely) and can't talk anymore. You won't be lying because sometimes you *are* busy—doing the laundry; just don't tell him you're doing the laundry. Never let him think, even if it's true, that you are home thinking about him and making the wedding guest list. Men love the seemingly unattainable girl!

Lest you think this advice is old-fashioned, remind yourself that you are a very fulfilled person—stable, functional, and happy—with a career, friends, and hobbies, and that you are perfectly capable of living with or without him. You are not an empty vessel waiting for him to fill you up, support you, or give you a life. You are alive and enthusiastic, engaged in work and in living fully on your own. Men like women who are their own person, not needy leeches waiting to be rescued. *The Rules* are not about being rescued!

In fact, the biggest mistake a woman can make

when she meets a man she wants to marry is to make him the center of her life. She may jeopardize her job by daydreaming at her desk about Prince Charming rather than rolling up her sleeves and working. All she thinks about and talks about is him. She bores her girlfriends to death with details about every date. She is constantly looking for ties to buy him or clipping newspaper articles that he would find interesting. Not only is such behavior unhealthy, but also it's the surest way to lose him.

First of all, he may be overwhelmed by all the attention. Second, he may never propose. And third, he may never rescue you emotionally and financially in the way you think. Even if he marries you, he may always have that night out with the boys, his hobbies, or that Sunday morning basketball game. And he may want a working wife. So better get used to the idea now that you *must* have a life of your own — a job, interests, hobbies, friends that you can fill up on in between dates and even when you are married. The worst thing you can do when dating is to expect him to be your entertainment director. Don't call him just because you're bored or want attention. Be happy and busy. He should always be catching you coming or going.

We hear again and again about women whose worlds shrink when they meet Mr. Right. When you meet Mr. Right is precisely the time to take up tennis, get an MBA, or go on that camping trip with your friends.

Rule #7

Don't Accept a Saturday Night Date after Wednesday

*I*t's quite common these days for men to ask women out for the same night or the very next day. And it's equally common for women to accept such casual, last-minute invitations out of fear that it will be the best offer they get that week. But this is not a *Rules* date. The man who eventually wants to marry you will not wait until the last minute to ask you out. On the contrary, he is kind, considerate, thoughtful and also afraid that if he doesn't pin you down five days in advance, he may not see you for another week. And when he is in love with you, a week will feel like eternity!

Needless to say, men don't always know that they shouldn't be calling you on Thursday or Friday night for a Saturday night date. Other women have spoiled them by accepting last-minute offers. As we've stated, ideally he should ask you out at the end of your last date or call you as early as Monday or Tuesday for the next Saturday night. *The Rules* will make you foremost on his mind, the first thing he thinks about in the morning. And if you are always on his mind, he won't want to wait until Thursday to call you.

It may be a telltale sign of how a man feels about you if he doesn't call you early in the week. The best way to encourage him to phone sooner is to turn him down when he calls on Thursday for Saturday night. Hopefully, he will get the hint. This is not a game. It is essential that men ask you out early in the week because, as a *Rules* woman, you simply can't put your life on hold until Thursday or Friday! You have friends and lots of things to do. You need to know ahead of time if you're going to have a date Saturday night or go to the movies with the girls. When men are calling you as late as Thursday, you become a nervous wreck. You're frenetically checking your answering machine, or if you live at home, you're constantly asking your mother if he called. Basically, you're living on the edge. *Rules* girls don't live on the edge. They have plans.

If he hasn't called by Wednesday night, make other plans for the weekend. Then you must politely decline if he calls Thursday and nonchalantly asks, "Hey, hon, what are you doing Saturday night?"

Practice the following answer in the nicest voice possible: "Oh, I'm so sorry, but I've already made plans." Don't break down and go out with him even though you'd much rather do that than hang out with the girls or go out with another man you don't like as much. And don't counteroffer by saying, "But I'm free Monday." Men have to ask you out without your help. *But don't reprimand him for calling so late in the week*. Be very nice, but very firm when you say no. Also, don't say what your plans are because it doesn't matter. What matters is the message you're sending, which is: If you want to get a Saturday night date with me, you must call on Monday, Tuesday or Wednesday.

Now you may be saying to yourself, "This is all so rigid, lots of men make plans when the mood strikes them, what's wrong with spontaneity?" These arguments sound convincing, but the reality is not so pleasant. When Ted first called our friend Beth on a Thursday night for a Saturday night date, she said yes right away. That set a bad precedent for him calling her at the last minute for future dates. Although they went out for a few months, he never thought that much about her during the week and she felt confused by the relationship because she was never sure if she was going to see him Saturday night.

Remember, *The Rules* are about the long haul. The way a man behaves—rather, the way you *allow* him to behave toward you—during your courtship is usually the way he will behave during your marriage. For example, if he's last minute about dating you, he'll be last minute and inattentive about you in other ways. That's why last-minute dates are just unacceptable. Men who call ten minutes before they're going to be in your neighborhood to see you may be terrific dates, but how busy and hard to get are you if they can see you in ten minutes? If you give in, these men will end up treating you like someone they *can get* in ten minutes.

But remember to be very nice when you say no. Don't think negatively, "This man doesn't think much of me to call right before he wants to see me," or scream, "No, I'm busy," and slam down the phone. He isn't thinking that at all. He isn't thinking that he's not treating you like a creature unlike any other. Give him a break. *Rules* girls are an unusual breed. As we've suggested, nicely say, "No, wow, I wish I wasn't busy!" Then sigh and get off the phone. He will soon realize that you simply want to be asked in advance for a date. Again, men are not trying to hurt you when they call at the last minute. Don't be offended, just train them to call earlier without actually *demanding* it of them.

Spontaneity is not "Hi. Want to see a movie this afternoon?" That call might have come out of boredom or the fact that the woman he really wants to be with is busy. He didn't call you in advance, dream about you for a week, and get all excited about putting his arm around your shoulders during the movie. He didn't think of your date together as something precious that must be scheduled in advance like a reservation at a very exclusive restaurant. Spontaneity is fine, but it should happen *during* the date, such as an unexpected drive to the beach after dinner.

We often hear about "spontaneous" women who go out with men on twenty-four hours' notice. We wish them luck. When a man knows he can have you five minutes after his last girlfriend gave him the boot, he'll call you because he's lonely or bored, not because he's crazy about you. In such cases, buyer beware: it won't last. Free spirits might object to what we are saying, but for long-lasting results we believe in treating dating like a job, with rules and regulations. Just like you have to work from nine to five, no matter how you *feel*, we believe you have to silently train men to make plans with you (elusive, busy, happy you!) ahead of time. When you do *The Rules*, what you're really doing is giving men the secret, silent code that they understand very well. If you make it too easy for men, they're certain to take advantage and then you can forget about getting a *Rules* marriage.

We realize that the days in between dates with the man you are crazy about can be long and excruciating; but, remember, it's worse to say yes indiscriminately whenever he wants to see you and risk him getting bored. If you play your cards right, he will reach the conclusion that the only way to see you whenever he wants, at the last minute, is to marry you!

Fill Up Your Time before the Date

*M*ost women go on dates with a lot of expectations. They want the man to find them beautiful, to ask them out again, and to father their children. Needless to say, these women are usually disappointed. That's why we have found it very helpful—in fact, essential—to be booked up as much as possible before the date. It's best to be busy right up until the doorbell rings so that you're slightly breathless and brimming with energy when you finally see him.

Here are some suggestions for what to do on the day of the date:

1. To relieve anxiety, go to the gym, get a manicure, or take a long hot bubble bath.

2. Buy a new shirt or a bottle of perfume. Get a makeover. Treat yourself.

3. Take a nap. If you're the type who gets drowsy at 10 P.M., a good nap will keep you going.

4. Go to the movies (see a comedy, not a romance, so love isn't too much on your mind), read the newspaper or a book to fill your head with something other than how your first name sounds with his last name. If you're busy all day, you won't be so needy and empty when he picks you up.

Here's what *not* to do:

1. Don't talk to your girlfriends all day long about the date, about how his astrological sign and yours go together, about how you know he's "The One," or about relationships in general. You really shouldn't be thinking about the date at all.

2. Don't see your mother, grandmother, or anyone who absolutely can't wait for you to get married and have children. Being around them might make you reek of desperation on the date. You might inadvertently mention the *M* word (marriage) and scare him away.

3. Don't write your name and his in all different combinations, such as:

> Susan Johnson
> Susan Dobbs Johnson
> Susan D. Johnson

Don't you have better things to do?

How to Act on Dates 1, 2, and 3

*I*f you are anything like us, you've thought a lot about how much the two of you have in common before he even arrives to pick you up. And you've named the children before he says hello. This type of seemingly innocuous daydreaming before the date is dangerous, possibly the worst thing you can do short of professing love to him during dessert. This kind of fantasizing leads to unfulfilled longing and to unrealistic expectations of romance and passion that makes you prone to say foolish things like, "I have two tickets to a concert," after the first date. (Yes, you can reciprocate but much later—see *Rule #4*).

If at all possible, don't think of him before he arrives—it isn't necessary for the first three dates. Be busy right up until the minute he buzzes you from downstairs. (Don't have him come up to your apartment on the first date. Preferably, meet him in the lobby of your apartment building or at a restaurant. *Rules* girls play it safe.) On these three dates, don't tell him all about your day as if you've known each other for years, thinking that it will bring you closer. Don't be too serious, controlling, or wifey. Don't mention the *M* word, not even to mention that your brother recently got married.

Remember that you are a creature unlike any other, a beautiful woman, inside and out. So don't feel that you have to fit in a love seminar or last-minute therapy session to be in good form. You should feel no pressure whatsoever.

In fact, all you really have to do on the first three dates is show up, relax, pretend you're an actress making a cameo appearance in a movie. Reread *Rule #1: Be a "Creature Unlike Any Other."* Be sweet and light. Laugh at his jokes, but don't try too hard. Smile a lot, and don't feel obligated to fill up the lulls in the conversation. In general, let him do all the work — pick you up, pick the restaurant, open the door, and pull out your chair. Act nonchalantly at all times, as if you're always on dates and it's nothing out of the ordinary (even if you haven't had a date in years). If you have to think about something, think about your date with another man that week. You should always try to date other people so that you never get hung up on one man at any time.

End the date first (see *Rule #11*), especially if you

like him. Glance at your watch after two hours (for a drink date) or three or four hours (for a dinner date), simply sigh, and say, "Gee, this was really great, but I've got a really big day tomorrow." Don't say what it is you're doing tomorrow. At the end of the first date, you can accept a light peck on the cheek or lips even though you're dying to do more.

Don't invite him up to your place at the end of the first date. After all, he's still a stranger at this point. He should only see the lobby of your apartment building. This is both for safety and *The Rules*. By not letting him into your apartment or agreeing to go to his, you drastically reduce your chances of any sort of problem occurring. If you meet someone at a bar or party, the same rule applies. Don't get into his car for any reason (or you might end up in his trunk!). Don't invite him to go to your apartment or go to his that night. It's a crazy world out there. Play it safe!

On the second date, use your judgment. If you feel comfortable with this man, he can pick you up at your apartment and you can invite him up for a drink at the end of the night. But when in doubt, meet him in the lobby of your building and say good night there as well. *Rules* girls don't take chances!

We know we're asking you to go against your feelings here, but you want to get married, don't you? Anyone can get a one-night stand. In summary, the first three dates should be like "being and nothingness." Dress nice, be nice, good-bye and go home. Not too much feeling, investment, or heart. You're probably wondering how long you can keep up this act, right? Don't worry, it gets easier!

How to Act on Dates 4
through Commitment Time

On the first three dates, you showed up and acted sweet. On the fourth date, you can show more of yourself. You can talk about your feelings, as long as you don't get too heavy, or play therapist or mother. Exhibit warmth, charm, and heart. If his dog died or his baseball team lost, express sympathy. Look into his eyes, be attentive and a good listener so that he knows you are a caring human being—a person who would make a supportive wife. Still, don't mention words like *marriage, wedding, kids,* or *the future.* Those are subjects for *him* to bring up. He *must* take the lead. Talk about something outside your relationship, like your favorite sport, TV show, a great movie, the novel you just finished, an interesting article from Sunday's *New*

York Times, or a good museum exhibition you just saw. You get the idea!

Don't tell him what your astrologist, nutritionist, personal trainer, shrink, or yoga instructor think about your relationship with him.

Don't tell him what a mess you were before you discovered seminars and gurus, as in, "My life was *such* a mess before The Forum (or est)."

Don't tell him he's the first man to treat you with respect. He'll think you're a loser or a tramp.

Don't give him the third degree about his past relationships. It's none of your business.

Don't say, "We've got to talk" in a serious tone, or he'll bolt from the bar stool.

Don't overwhelm him with your career triumphs. Try to let *him* shine.

Don't plague him with your neuroses!!

Remember, you won't have to keep such things to yourself forever. Just for the first few months . . . until he says he's in love with you. Eventually you will become more of yourself. It's the first impressions from the first few months of dating that men remember forever.

If you find it hard to keep up this act, then end the date early or see less of him. Letting it all hang out too soon is counterproductive to your goals. Many women are conditioned in therapy to open up very soon. This is fine for therapy or with a girlfriend, but don't do this on a date. *The Rules* are about opening up slowly so that men aren't overwhelmed by us. It's rather selfish and inconsiderate to burden people with our whole lives on a three-hour date, don't you think? Remember, *The Rules* are innately unselfish.

But not so unselfish that you feel you have to answer any question you regard as too personal or none of his business just yet. Don't tell him anything that you will regret. Some men like to pry secrets out of women. Women sometimes reveal more than they really care to, hoping that their revelations will draw a man closer to them—but afterwards they feel naked, as well as tricked and cheated. Better to smile when asked a question that is too personal, and say, "Oh, I'd rather not talk about that right now."

Of course, personal matters may come up. Be careful how you answer his questions. If he asks you how long you are planning to live in your apartment, say you're renewing your lease. Don't say, for example, that you've been hoping to meet a man soon so that you can get a bigger apartment with him when your lease is up. Even if that is in fact your true hope and desire, don't say so or your date will run to the nearest exit.

Act independent so that he doesn't feel that you're expecting him to take care of you. That's as true on the first date as the fiftieth. Jill remembers that when she went bed shopping for herself with Bruce, her boyfriend of six months, she deliberately bought a single bed rather than a queen-size bed. It killed her to have to do this as she was hoping he was "The One" and knew if they were to get engaged and married she would have no use for the bed. But the fold-out couch she'd been sleeping on was broken. Rather than consulting Bruce on the bed purchase—asking him what kind of bed he liked and what size he liked, as if to suggest that this might be the bed they would be sharing one day—she bought the single bed as if she had no intention of getting married soon.

It was important not to let Bruce know that she was buying a bed with him in mind, when they weren't married and might never be. Of course, the single bed hasn't gone to waste: Jill's in-laws (Bruce's parents) now keep it as a spare in their guest room.

Always End the Date First

*I*f you have not been living by *The Rules*, then you probably didn't know that the first date or two should last no more than five hours. A good way to end the date is to nonchalantly glance at your watch and say something like, "Gosh, I really must be going now. I have such a busy day tomorrow." (As we said before, don't say what you're doing. It doesn't matter and it's none of his business.)

Ending the date first is not so easy when you really like him and want to marry him, and you're both having a great time. But it must be done because you must leave him wanting more of you, not less. If he wants to know more about you as the date is ending, he can always call you the next day or ask you out again when he drops you off. It is our experience that men will want to see you a lot, sometimes every day in the beginning, and then grow very bored very quickly. So abide by *The Rules* and he'll stay smitten.

Not ending the date first is bad enough. What's *worse*, however, is prolonging the date once it should have been over. Randy felt that she was "losing" Bob at the end of their second date (dinner and movie), so she suggested that they go dancing. Bob didn't want to hurt her feelings so he said okay, then he never called again. Of course, Randy should have ended the date right after the movie, but she thought she could excite Bob with her great disco dancing.

Other women try to prolong a first or second date, for example, by inviting the man up to her apartment for a drink or coffee so that he'll fall in love with her decorating, or her home-brewed decaf. No! First of all, it should be *the man* trying to prolong the date, not you. He should be suggesting dancing, drinks, or a café where the two of you can get dessert and cappuccino. If he didn't suggest it, then it's not supposed to happen. Instead of worrying about making the date interesting or longer, just make sure you end it first.

Rule #12 _____

Stop Dating Him if He Doesn't Buy You a Romantic Gift for Your Birthday or Valentine's Day

*W*hat kind of present can you expect to receive on your birthday when a man is in love with you? Ideally, jewelry, but any romantic gift will do. Now don't get us wrong. This is not a rule for gold diggers; it's just that when a man wants to marry you, he usually gives you jewelry, not sporty or practical gifts like a toaster oven or coffee maker. It is not how expensive the item is, but the *type* of gift it is. A typewriter can cost more than an inexpensive pair of earrings, and a computer, one would think, connotes love, being such a costly item; but such presents come from the head, not the heart, and are not good signs of love at all. Therefore, *The Rule* is that if you don't get jewelry or some other romantic gift on your birthday or other significant occasion, you might as well call it quits because he's not in love with you and chances are you won't get the most important gift of all: an engagement ring.

No one knows this rule better than Susan, who received a Sergio Tacchini sweat suit for Valentine's Day from Brian, her boyfriend of three months. When we told her the romance was over, she argued that the suit costs almost two hundred dollars and is very cool at the better country clubs. But we knew that Susan would have been better off with candy or flowers. Why? Because even though Brian's gift was expensive, it was not romantic. When men are in love, they give love objects even if they are on a tight budget. Flowers, jewelry, poetry, and weekend trips to the country are the kinds of gifts given by men in love. Sweat suits, books, briefcases, toasters, and other practical gifts are the kinds of things men give when they like you, care about you (like a sister), but don't really want to marry you. (Sure enough, Brian dropped Susan a few months later.)

Remember, gift giving has nothing to do with money. We know a poor student who could only afford a $1.50 greeting card for his girlfriend on Valentine's Day. He then spent four hours writing a beautiful love poem to her in it. A *Rules* present if there ever was one! As most women know, the time a man spends on anything is virtually priceless.

One more point about greeting cards: check to see if he signs "love." A man may sometimes send a greeting card with very casual intentions. If he doesn't sign it "love," don't assume he does. When Bobby was dating Cheryl, he signed his cards, "Yours, Bobby." (I just *know* he loves me, she'd tell her friends.) They eventually had "a talk," and he told her he wasn't in love with her. So don't assume anything. Just read what's written!

Furthermore, while a romantic gift is a must for birthdays, Valentine's Day, and anniversaries, a man who is crazy about you will give you all kinds of things all the time. You're always on his mind, so you might get a stuffed animal he sees at a street fair or something kooky that's just perfect for you. For example, when Patty expressed an interest in biking, her boyfriend Mike bought her a fancy helmet. If he didn't love her, he would have given her the helmet on her birthday, but being in love, he gave her a necklace and flowers on her birthday and the helmet to celebrate their six-month anniversary.

When you do receive gifts, don't overreact. When Lori received roses from Kevin on their third date she was absolutely ecstatic. She rarely had gotten flowers from anyone she liked, but she did *The Rules* thing to do, she smiled, nonchalantly put them in a vase, and said, "Thank you!"

In general, *The Rule* is that when a man loves you he just wants to give you things. Anything. If your glass is empty in a restaurant, he wants to give you water or promptly asks the waiter to get it. If you can't see the screen in the movie theater, he asks five people to move over to give you another seat. If he sees you digging in your bag for a pen, he lends you his and then tells you to keep it. Basically, he notices everything about you, except anything bad. If you're ten pounds overweight, he doesn't think you're overweight, he thinks you're cute. But if your girlfriend (whom he is not in love with) is the same size, he thinks *she's* fat. When a man is not in love with you, he notices nothing or only the bad. For example, he might say, "Lose weight and I'll take you on vacation." You feel you have to earn his love. That's not *The Rules*, that's conditional love and not what we're after.

Again, this is not about being gold diggers or princesses wanting to be doted on all the time. It's about determining whether a man is truly in love with you and, if not, going on to the next. If you end up marrying a man who gives you a briefcase instead of a bracelet on your birthday, you may be doomed to a life of practical, loveless gifts and gestures from him such as food processors, and you may spend thousands of dollars in therapy trying to figure out why there's no romance in your marriage.

Don't See Him More than Once or Twice a Week

*M*ost men fall in love faster than women. They also fall *out* of love faster. They may want to see you two or three times a week, some even every day, in the beginning. If you give in and see them every time, eventually they get restless and irritable, and then stop calling. They seem moody a lot and say things like, "I don't know what's wrong. I just have a lot going on right now."

To keep a man from getting too much too soon, don't see him more than once or twice a week for the first month or two. Let him think you have "other plans," that he is not the only man or interest in your life. When we hear someone say that she just met the greatest man and sees him every day, we think, "Uh oh, this isn't going to turn out so well." A woman *must* pace the relationship slowly. Don't expect a man to do it.

We know how painful this can be. It's only natural that when you meet a man you like who also likes you, you want to see him all the time. You want to know all about him—his favorite color, his past relationships, what he eats for breakfast, everything—almost overnight. So it's hard for you to say no when he asks you out for Saturday night, Sunday brunch, and a Monday night dinner and movie all in one breath. But, girls, you must put your foot down! Don't make seeing you so easy. Men like sports and games—football, tennis, blackjack, and poker—because they love a challenge. So be a challenge!

Remember, this *Rule* is not forever. After seeing him once a week for the first month, you can see him twice or three times a week during the second month, and three to four times a week in the third month. But never more than four or five times a week unless you're engaged. Men must be conditioned to feel that if they want to see you seven days a week they have to marry you. And until that blessed proposal occurs, you must practice saying no to extra dates even though you're dying to spend more time with him and even though you've mentally said to yourself, "This is The One."

If, for example, after kissing you passionately at the end of your first or second date he says, "So what are you doing tomorrow?," summon up your sweetest voice and say, "I'm sorry. I already have plans."

Stick to your ground, even if you feel intoxicated by the smell of his cologne on your neck. And, of course, don't say what your plans are or include him in them.

A man who is in love with you and hopes to marry you won't be put off by the once-to-twice-a-week dating structure you set up in the beginning. We find that only men who are just with you for fun or sex are likely to get angry or impatient. Don't be fooled if these men say the kinds of things that make you believe they want to marry you. It happens all the time. It's called Standard Operating Procedure.

On the first date, such a man might point to a restaurant and say, "That's where my father proposed to my mother," leading you to think that he will propose to you there one day. Or he might talk about the future, saying something like, "In the summer we can go to Connecticut and I'll take you to this great seafood place." You are naturally in heaven, thinking that this man has plotted out your lives forever. It might all be true and he may call again and ask you out. But it might be a ploy to get you into bed on the first or second date.

If you fall for his lines and see him every night that week—after all, you think he is serious about you—he might take you out a couple of times and have sex with you. But he may never call again or worse, he may continue to date you, but you'll end up watching his interest fade away. (A very painful thing. Watching someone falling "out of love" is really awful!) If you follow *The Rules* and slow down the process, forcing him to get to know you and *really* fall in love, this will not happen.

The Rules will make you harder to get so that a man who doesn't really like you won't waste his or your time. So do yourself a favor and do *The Rules*. Don't see him more than once or twice a week!

No More than Casual Kissing on the First Date

*I*t's common knowledge that men want as much as they can get on the first date. It's your job to slow them down. Let him kiss you on the first date, but nothing more. Keeping it to a kiss will force him not to think of you as just a physical object. If a *Rules* relationship is to develop, he must fall in love with your soul, your whole being, not just your body. So the less you do physically, the better. Besides, it's easier to stop something if you don't let things get too hot and heavy right away.

We know this is not an easy *Rule* to follow, particularly when you're out with someone really cute and he's driving fast in his sports car and kissing you at every red light. He's a great kisser and you wonder what else he's great at. This is when you have to brace yourself and say, "*The Rule* is no more than casual kissing on the first date. No, don't invite him up to the apartment. No, don't let his hands go everywhere." If you're getting too excited, end the date quickly so you don't do anything you'll regret. If he wants more of you, let him call you and ask you for a second date.

Some men might make you feel that you're being old-fashioned or prudish. Some might make fun of you or even get angry. Let them know as nicely as you can that if they don't like it, they can get lost! If a man pressures you, then he's not someone you want to date. Keep telling yourself that other women have spoiled men by sleeping with them on the first date, but you're a *Rules* girl and you take your time. If he really cares about you, he will respect your boundaries. If he's a gentleman, he'll let the physical part of the relationship develop at your pace and never force anything on you. Forget all the "free love" theories from the swinging sixties. Besides, it's not spontaneous or cool to have an unwanted pregnancy or a disease.

In addition, if you are following *Rule #9: (How to Act on Dates 1, 2, and 3)*, things should not get out of hand. As we said earlier, you should be talking about politics, real estate, good movies, not marriage, kids, love, former boyfriends and girlfriends, and sexual positions. The conversation should be cordial, not steamy, so you don't end up in bed after dessert. Besides, if you really like him, just kissing can be a lot of fun!

Don't Rush into Sex and Other *Rules* for Intimacy

When is it okay to have sex? *The Rule* depends on your age and personal feelings. If you're eighteen and a virgin, you will want to wait until you are in a committed relationship. If you're thirty-nine, waiting a month or two can be fine. Of course, if you feel strongly against premarital sex, you should wait until you're married. If he loves you, he'll respect *whatever* decision you make.

But don't be surprised if the man you're dating gets very angry when you kiss him good night in the lobby at the end of your second date rather than invite him up to your apartment for a drink. He has probably been spoiled by other women who slept with him on the first or second date and now he feels he's being denied this pleasure. But don't worry.

Anger indicates interest, and you might be surprised, for he will probably call you again!

But what if you like sex a lot too, and denying yourself is just as hard as denying him? Does that mean you can sleep with him on the first or second date? Unfortunately, the answer is still no. You will just have to exercise a bit of self-restraint and character building here and trust that if you hold off for a few weeks or months, you won't be sorry. Why risk having him call you easy (and think of you that way) when he's talking to his buddies in the locker room the next day? Better that he be angry and strategizing ways of seducing you on the next date than moving onto the next girl. Making him wait will only increase his desire and create more passion when you finally have sex whenever you're ready.

We know it can be excruciating to put sex off with someone you're attracted to, but you must think long term here. If you play your cards right, you can have sex with him every night for the rest of your life when you're married!

Now you might argue that you don't mind having sex with him on the first or second date and taking your chances, that it's okay with you if he doesn't call again because you're both grown-ups and you can take your lumps. We know from experience, of course, that most girls who say this are lying to themselves. Deep down inside it's not okay with a woman if she sleeps with a man and he doesn't call. Every woman wants the man she just slept with to call her, that is, if she really likes him—and hopefully she likes the man she's sleeping with. Every woman we know who said it was okay if a man didn't call after sex was actually *not okay* when he didn't call. When you sleep with him on the second date, you don't really know if he's going to be a gentleman or a creep. *Rules* girls don't take risks. We wait until we're sure before having sex.

Let's say that now, hopefully, you've held off for a while and are ready to have sex with him. What *Rules* should you follow in bed? First and foremost, stay emotionally cool no matter how hot the sex gets. The fact is, most women turn men off not only because they sleep with them too soon, but because they talk too much about it in bed. They try to exploit the physical closeness of sex to gain emotional closeness, security, and assurances about the future. The theories of Masters and Johnson (who are now divorced) are not to be ignored, but please wait a good amount of time before you begin holding lengthy seminars about your needs during sex or after sex. Don't be a drill sergeant, demanding that he do this or that. You have to trust that if you relax and let him explore your body like unchartered territory you will have fun and be satisfied. Being with you in bed should not be difficult or demanding. Don't bring anything—red lightbulbs, scented candles, or X-rated videos—to enhance your sexual experience. If you have to use these things to get him excited, something's wrong. He should be excited about just sleeping with you.

While you're snuggling in bed after great sex is not the time to say, "So, do you want me to make room in the closet for your clothes?" or "I put a toothbrush in the bathroom for you." Don't bring up marriage, kids, or your future together, not in bed (or out). Remember, these are *your* needs you are concerned about filling, and *The Rules* are a selfless way of living and handling a relationship. Men merely want to lie down next to someone they care about when they are feeling strong emotions. Women are more curious, wanting to know, "Now that we've slept together, where is this relationship going?" or "What is the meaning of what we've just done?" While all these thoughts are whirling through your head and your desire to own this man is mounting from minute to minute, try to relax and think about nothing.

Don't cling to him if he has to leave that night or the following morning. Be casual and unmoved about the fact that the date is over. With that attitude, chances are he will be the one hanging on. Don't try to keep him there longer by suggesting brunch or sweet rolls and coffee in bed. If you do, he'll probably run to the nearest coffee shop for breakfast. Instead, go quietly about your business — brush your hair and your teeth, do some sit-ups and stretches, brew coffee — and chances are he'll start massaging your shoulders and suggesting morning sex or a great brunch place.

It's only fair that if you're dating a man for a month or two and don't plan to sleep with him for a while to let him know. Otherwise, you're being a tease. On the other hand, what if *you're* more into sex than he is? *The Rules* answer is, if you don't want to feel insecure, then don't initiate sex. After you're in a committed relationship, when you know he is crazy about you, you can occasionally and playfully make an overture.

Last but not least, whenever you do have sex, always use a condom. Don't cave in when a man says, "Just this once." Remember, you're a *Rules* girl and you take good care of yourself.

Don't Tell Him What to Do

*I*f your boyfriend wants to join the new "in" health club where all the leggy model types work out, don't tell him to jog on the street or exercise at home. Say, "That's great!" and go about your business. Don't show that you are jealous or insecure. If he loves you, it won't matter how pretty the girls at the gym are.

If he'd rather go camping with his friends on the weekends than be with you, either let him or break up with him, but don't tell him what to do. Our friend Marcy was seeing Joe for a couple of months when he suddenly started to make weekend plans with his friends. Conditioned by her therapist to be honest and up front about her feelings, Marcy told Joe that she felt abandoned. He immediately started making weekend plans with her. She was ecstatic. But after a month of togetherness, he suddenly stopped calling. She never heard from him again.

The moral of the story: don't play social director. If Joe didn't want to spend weekends with Marcy, being asked to wasn't going to change his mind. Men do what they want to do. If they can't live without you, it's very clear. If they can live without you, it's also clear. Don't be dense. Read the tea leaves and move on to the next man if necessary!

If, after dating you for months, he has never introduced you to his parents or friends, that means he doesn't want you to meet his parents or friends. He may simply be shy about the whole thing. Don't be pushy and suggest meeting them if he doesn't bring it up. We don't force ourselves on the family. We don't make friends with his roommate or take his mother to lunch so that she'll tell him to marry us. No one can make him marry us. Either accept the situation as it is and be patient, or date others, but don't force anything to happen.

Finally, don't try to change his life in any way. Don't go through his closets and throw out his favorite but disgusting old jeans and then suggest you and he go shopping for new ones. Don't try to turn him on to tennis when he loves drinking beer and watching football. Don't sign him up for career counseling courses because *you're* unhappy with his current job. Don't push your interests on him either. If he loves steak, don't preach the virtues of vegetarianism. You don't own him. Don't fix him. You will end up emasculating him and he will come to see you as a domineering shrew. He wants someone who makes him feel good or better, not inadequate. So leave him alone. When he *asks* you what to wear or how to play tennis, you can help him. Until then, just be there.

Let Him Take the Lead

*D*ating is like slow dancing. The man must take the lead or you fall over your feet. He should be the first one to say "I love you," "I miss you," "I've told my parents so much about you. They can't wait to meet you."

He should be an open book, you should be a mystery. Don't tell him he's the first person you've felt this way about in a long time, or that you never thought you'd fall in love again.

Remember, let him take the lead. He declares love first, just as he picks most of the movies, the restaurants, and the concerts the two of you go to. He might sometimes ask you for your preference, in which case you can tell him.

You should meet his parents before he meets yours

unless, of course, he picks you up at your parents' house. Let your mother or father open the door, but don't let them hang around too much. Tell your mother not to smile at him as if he were her son-in-law and don't let her mention your sister's upcoming wedding. Remember, mothers can get quite anxious about your dating life. So be ready to go—don't be in the bathroom applying more mascara—when he arrives so that your parents don't spend too much time with him alone, asking him questions like, "How's business?" or "So what are your intentions?"

The same rule applies to your friends. He should introduce you to his friends before you introduce him to yours. You should double with his married or dating friends before you double with yours.

Reciprocate when you feel quite secure about the way the relationship is going and don't tell your friends too much about him because they might inadvertently blab when they do meet him. If you can't trust them to be quiet and discreet, then say nothing. The last thing you need is a well-meaning, but not too smart friend, saying something like, "Oh, it's nice to meet you. Sheila has told me *so* much about you."

Don't worry. After he proposes, he will eventually meet all your friends and family. Until then, just follow his lead!

Rule #18

Don't Expect a Man to Change or Try to Change Him

*L*et's say you have met the man of your dreams—almost. There are a couple of things you wish were different. What do you do? Nothing! Don't try to change him because men never *really* change. You should either accept certain flaws or find someone else. Of course, it all depends on what it is about him that bothers you.

If he is fanatically neat, chronically tardy, hates Chinese food (your favorite) and disco dancing (you love it), or he won't part with his childhood baseball card collection, but he loves you to death, consider yourself lucky. These are annoying but relatively harmless vices, which we classify under category A.

On the other hand, if he flirts with other women in front of you at parties, exhibits violent behavior at times, pays no attention when you are telling him something important, or forgets your birthday, then he is into category B (bad) behavior and you have some heavy-duty thinking to do.

In the case of A, pray for acceptance and don't nag him. It won't work anyway. Just be ready at 9 P.M. when he says he'll be over at 8.

When it comes to B-type behavior, such as infidelity and lack of consideration, seriously think about ending the relationship. People don't change that much and you can't *count* on it happening. What you see is what you get. If a man cheated on you during your courtship, he may do so during your marriage. He might be on best behavior for a while after you catch him the first time. But don't delude yourself. Old habits die hard.

You must decide if you can live with him. Whether or not he ever cheats on you again, realize that the thought will always cross your mind. You might find yourself checking his shirt collar for lipstick stains and his pockets for little pieces of paper with women's phone numbers on them, or calling him at the office when he says he's working late. Is that how you want to live? If it is, *Rules* women make up their minds and live with it. The key to a successful marriage is to be happy with the way things are, not the way they could be *if only* he changed.

Of course, a playboy type who falls in love with you because you did *The Rules* will automatically mend his ways. He will want to be monogamous because you, unlike other women he's dated, are busy, don't call him, make him wait for sex, and don't bring up marriage or the future. Therefore, his object in life is to win you over. He has very little interest in other women because he has no time for them! Thoughts of how to conquer you consume most of his waking hours. You have become the biggest challenge in his life. Do *The Rules* and even the biggest playboy can be all yours!

Deciding whether or not you can live with a man's bad habits or his past (ex-wives and children) is not easy. Also, some character traits don't fall so easily into either category A or B. For example, your man may be someone who doesn't live up to his earning potential. Whether you can live with him depends on how important money, career, status, and a big house are to you.

In all such cases, you must sit quietly with yourself and ask for guidance to do the right thing. Consulting others helps, but remember *you* have to live with these things yourself. Ask yourself if you can really marry an ex-womanizer or a recovering alcoholic. Can you really live with the possibility that he may cheat or drink again? Ask yourself if you can live with stepchildren or past infidelity. If the answer is yes, great. But if you are too troubled by his past or current behavior, you might have to do *The Rules* thing and walk away. Taking him to couples therapy in the hopes of changing him can take forever, rarely works, and some things just cannot be changed.

Whatever you do, don't nag him or he's sure to resent you for it. So think long and hard, but don't waste too much time deciding. Remember, there are lots of men out there!

Don't Open Up Too Fast

*D*ating is not therapy. There are many ways to kill a relationship. Getting heavy and examining everything is certainly one of them. Conditioned by therapy and self-help books to tell all, women tend to overdo it on first dates, bringing up past relationships, their hurts and fears, their alcohol or drug problem—all in an attempt to bond with this new man. This is deadly and boring. Be intelligent but light, interesting yet mysterious. That's why we have suggested not opening up too fast. (See also *Rule #9: How to Act on Dates 1, 2, and 3.*) The first date should be short, so you don't say too much. Remember, the person who talks the most has the most to lose.

By the end of the first date, he should know just a

few facts, such as your name, your profession, how many siblings you have, where you went to college, where you grew up, and your favorite restaurants. By the end of the first date, he should not know your dating history. Don't reprimand him for picking you up thirty minutes late and then tell him you were afraid he would never show up, that you felt abandoned, and explain that "abandonment" is one of your issues in therapy. Don't tell him that his behavior reminds you of your ex-boyfriend who was also never on time. Even if this is true, don't tell him. Don't worry. By doing *The Rules*, you will automatically attract a loving, attentive husband who will be around so much that you won't have time to think about your abandonment issues!

If you have a burning desire to tell him a secret, *The Rules* credo is "Haste makes waste." It's always better to wait before telling someone something that you might feel ashamed or nervous about. Wait at least a couple of months. Better yet, wait until after he says "I love you." Unless he loves you, it's none of his business anyway!

Too many women tell intimate details of their lives far too soon. This is not only unwise, but also it doesn't work. No man wants to be the recipient of a therapy session upon first meeting you. No man wants to hear how wrong or messed up your life has been before he *really* loves you.

You are not on this date to get sympathy but to have a nice evening and get him to call you again.

Remember *Rule #9*—that the first three dates are about being light and charming, like a summer breeze. Men must always remember you as mysterious on the first three dates. Their initial impression tends to go a long way. If and when things get serious, you can casually tell him about your difficult childhood and some of your fears. Even then, tell him in an easy, short, simple way. Don't be dramatic about your past. Don't go into long details. Don't be burdensome.

Let's say you are a recovering alcoholic. He takes you out for a drink on your first date and to dinner on the second. He notices you only ordered club soda both times. He is about to order a bottle of wine and wants to know if you'll join him. Don't say, "No, I *never* drink. I hit a terrible bottom with drugs and alcohol two years ago and now I'm sober in AA." Just say, "No, thanks," and smile. After a couple of months when he's madly in love with you and you feel that he would not judge you for your drinking problem, you can tell him something like, "I used to drink a lot in college. It really made me sick. Now I'm in AA and I don't drink anymore. I feel better." Then smile and go on to other, more pleasant conversation. If he loves you, he will not make you feel bad. He won't argue with you or try to encourage you to "just have one." He might even start drinking less himself to make you feel better. He might even say that he's proud of your sobriety and discipline.

If you've had a serious illness and you're embarrassed about obvious scars from your surgery, wait until you're about to be intimate with him and then casually mention, as you take your clothes off in the dark, that you had an illness. If he loves you, he will kiss and caress you. Don't bring up the illness in a serious, heart-to-heart talk on your first date. Remember, especially in the beginning, don't be too intense about anything or lay all your cards on the table. In general, the less tragic you are about your life circumstances, the more sympathy you will probably get. Ask for sympathy and you never get it.

If you don't know how to hold on to a dollar, don't balance your checkbook, have an answering machine filled with calls from bill collectors leaving threatening messages, don't tell him what a mess you are with finances and that you got it from your father who once gambled away your college tuition. Now you might feel that we are asking you to act casually about your problems, but the fact is, you are bad with money and he will soon see that. But does he really have to know about the creditors and your canceled credit cards? No, all he has to know is that money is not your strong suit.

We are not suggesting that you hide or lie about bad things in your life, just that you not burden him with all the gory details too soon. Does he really have to know that your last boyfriend dropped you for your best friend? Can't you just say, if he asks, that your last relationship "just didn't work out"?

He should always feel that he's in love with the

girl of his dreams, not someone damaged. If you *feel* damaged (many of us do in some way), read *Rule #1* again and again. Remember, you are a creature unlike any other! It's when and how you tell him your darkest secrets, not the secrets themselves, that matter.

By the time you are engaged, he should know *all* that really matters about you and your family and your past. *The Rules* are truthful and spiritual in nature. It is morally wrong to accept an engagement ring without revealing whatever truths about yourself you need to share. Tell him these things in a calm, nondramatic manner and don't, as some women do, surprise him with these skeletons after you're married. That's not the time to tell him that you were previously married or never finished college. It's not fair to him and not good for a *Rules* marriage.

Be Honest but Mysterious

*M*en love mystery! Fifty years ago it was easier to be mysterious with men. Women lived at home and their mothers answered the phone and never told the men who else called their daughters. Dates didn't see women's bedrooms so soon. Today, men pick up women at their apartments, see their lingerie in the bathroom, their romance novels in the living room, and hear their phone messages. While such openness is good for marriage, it's important to project a certain amount of mystery during the dating period.

We are all looking for someone to share our lives, thoughts, and feelings with, but as we suggested in *Rule #19* wait until he says he loves you to share your innermost secrets. When he is in your apartment, don't listen to your answering machine. Let him wonder who called you besides him! You might know that the messages are probably from girl-friends feeling suicidal about their dating situations, but he doesn't!

If your date is at your place and one of your friends calls and asks how everything is going, don't say, "*Scott*'s over. I can't talk." That means you've been talking about Scott to your friends and he's somehow important. Even if that is the case, Scott should not know that he is the subject of your thoughts and conversations or he might think he doesn't have to work so hard to get you. Simply say, "I can't talk right now. I'll call you later." After you hang up, don't tell him who called or why.

Before he comes to your apartment, tuck this book away in your top drawer and make sure any self-help books are out of sight. Have interesting or popular novels or nonfiction books in full view. Hide in the closet any grungy bathrobes or something you don't want him to see, such as a bottle of Prozac.

In general, don't give away any information that is not absolutely necessary. If you are busy on the night he asks you for a date, don't tell him what you are planning to do. Just say you are busy. If he asks you out for the weekend, don't say, "I'm visiting my brother this weekend. His wife just had a baby." Simply say, "I'm sorry, but I already have plans." Less is more. Let him wonder what you are doing. You don't have to be an open book. This is good for him and it's good for you. It keeps the intrigue going.

You don't want to make dating you so easy and predictable that he loses interest in you. Always remember that in time you will be able to tell him just about anything!

On the other hand, *Rules* girls don't lie either. Don't tell a Mel Gibson–type guy that you love hiking and shop at L.L. Bean all the time when you can't stand trees, insects, and backpacks. And certainly don't tell your boyfriend that you love and want children because he does when you really don't. Take our advice. Don't lie. It's a law of the universe.

Rule #21

Accentuate the Positive and Other *Rules* for Personal Ads

*P*ersonal ads have become a popular way to meet men. But many women shy away from ads because they feel it smacks of desperation. Don't worry! We know lots of women who've placed and answered ads without seeming desperate or too interested. That's because they wrote or responded to ads in a *Rules* way.

1. How to Write a Personal Ad

Ads can be expensive, so make yours no more than four or five lines. Ads that run on and on are a waste of money and seem desperate. (Why else would anyone spend six hundred dollars for one ad?) Not surprisingly, they contain too much information that no one cares about, and too much lovey-dovey stuff (of course you like walks on the beach, who doesn't?). Most people skim or ignore long ads and rarely respond to them. Think of advertising campaigns ("It takes a tough man to make a tender chicken," "Maybe she was born with it. Maybe it's Maybelline") when you write an ad. It should be short, upbeat, and flirtatious—a pleasure to read. It should contain facts only about height, hair color, religion, sex, and profession. Don't mention marriage or kids. Don't refer to your past—for example, divorced or newly available since your last breakup. Don't say things like, "I'm not into makeup or superficiality" or "I'm happily overweight." Perhaps a man will not mind your extra twenty pounds when he sees your beautiful face, but chances are he won't answer such a candid ad.

Many ads are a turnoff because they look for sympathy. The writers hope to hook you in by telling you that they are human and damaged. For example, "Ex-wife of alcoholic seeks nonabusive soul mate." It's honest but a bit depressing, don't you think? I mean, would you answer a man's ad that said, "Unemployed executive looking for understanding wife?" Thus, *The Rule* is that as long as you don't outright lie, you needn't be honest to a fault either. Just leave things out—for example, don't say you're slim if you're fat. Simply leave out your weight entirely and accentuate your blue eyes and long blond hair.

Don't be shy! It's perfectly okay to ask for exactly the kind of man you want. We know one woman who said only men with Porsches need apply. You might think she had a lot of nerve, or that men might be turned off by such an ad because the woman comes across as a gold digger. The fact is that this woman received dozens of letters with photos of men in front of their Porsches and she married one of them. Another woman wanted only the kind of man who would write poetry. Dozens of men sent her poems. Men like to be challenged in an ad and like impressing women, so let them. Ask for what you want—just don't say you want to get married.

When you receive responses, sort them out into yes, no, and maybe piles. Don't rule out letters without photos. Men are often lazy about such things. If you like their note and the sound of their voice on the phone, agree to a drink date. But be wary if a man doesn't mention certain critical facts in his letter. You don't want too many surprises on the first date.

2. How to Answer an Ad

Get some plain white stationery the size of a telephone memo pad, don't perfume it or seal it with a kiss and *never* include your address—you don't want any crazies stalking you at your apartment. (More about safety at the end of this chapter.) Write a flirtatious note with the essential facts. If his ad said, "Marriage-minded, Tom Cruise look-alike," you could start your note off with: "Dear Tom" or "Dear T.C." Never mention marriage, even though he brought it up in boldface.

Remember, you're just doing this for fun, to meet some nice men. Notes that talk about marriage, kids, and commitment make most men run the other way even when they want it. Just start out with something easy like, "Your ad caught my eye." (That makes it sound like you were casually reading XYZ magazine. He needn't know that your Monday night ritual is poring over personal ads looking for your husband or that you answered twenty other ads that week.)

Don't try to be different. Don't send a sleazy photo or a collage from a fashion magazine with your face over Cindy Crawford's body. All of that is sophomoric. It also shouts desperation. The best way to respond is to dash off a cute note in five minutes while watching the 11 o'clock news. Less is more. Remember, he has a lot of other letters to read. End the note by saying something like, "Well, I'm off to my aerobics class. Hope to hear from you soon." Keep it light!

The photo is actually the most important part of the package. Most men decide to call you based on your photo, not your note. They either like your looks or they don't, so spend the extra time getting the right photo. It should be about 3x5, no posters or photo-booth photos, preferably of you alone and smiling. Don't send photos of you holding your one-year-old niece or in a bikini or with a girlfriend.

Don't be surprised if you only get one or two replies for every twenty ads you respond to. Men typically receive hundreds of responses from women. Some take weeks and months to call. When you do get a call, try to make the date for only a quick drink. You have no idea what he looks like and he may have been exaggerating about how handsome he is. On the other hand, he could very well be Kevin Costner's twin. A short drink date will give you enough time to decide if he's for you, which is all that matters.

A word of caution: dating via personal ads involves taking risks that usually dating by introduction doesn't. You don't know this man from a hole in the wall! —so be careful! When he calls you to set up a date, don't feel you have to go out with him if he sounds weird, angry, or rude. But if you do like him and the sound of his voice, agree to meet at a restaurant near your apartment. *Never* give him your address or meet him at your apartment, and *never* let him pick you up in his car to drive to a restaurant. If he gets very angry because you won't let him pick you up at your apartment, or makes you feel that you're being paranoid, say "Maybe this isn't going to work out" and get off the phone. But if everything is okay, make sure to get his telephone number, saying you want it in case you need to cancel or reschedule.

Then call the number to make sure it's his. Hang up when he or his answering machine answers. Give your mother or a friend the number before the date so someone can track you down if anything happens. We know all this precaution seems very unromantic, but *Rules* girls don't take unnecessary risks!

Don't Live with a Man (or Leave Your Things in His Apartment)

*T*o live together or not to live together? Is that a question you're grappling with now? Your friends (not knowing *The Rules*) might say, "Do it." Your parents (being conservative) will no doubt say, "No." *The Rules* answer is: "Move in only if you've set a wedding date." In other words, the only reason to live with someone is if you're planning the wedding and you don't want to pay two rents.

Contrary to popular belief, living together is not a trial period for him to see how he feels about you. He either loves you or he doesn't, and playing house and cooking him a lot of breakfasts won't change a thing. In fact, sometimes the best way for him to see how he feels about you is to not see you at all. You may have to dump him if he can't commit. If he really loves you, he'll beg you to come back. If he doesn't, you've lost nothing, saved time, and can now go on to someone else.

Women who think that commitment will come *after* they shack up often learn the hard way that this is not the case. Of course, by the time the lesson is learned, their self-esteem is shattered and they're two or three or four years older. Does this scenario sound familiar? After dating Mitch for a year and a half, Wendy wanted a ring. Mitch wouldn't budge. They decided to live together to see if they could "work it out" (his idea and word choice). Nothing changed. When he went away on business trips he didn't call or think about her that much. Nine months and a lot of wasted time later, he was still not in love, and so he moved out. Wendy attributed the breakup to his parents' messy divorce, which he was working out in therapy. The truth is, she should have just ended it sooner when he wouldn't commit.

If you operate under the delusion that living together without a real commitment will somehow bring you closer together, you should know that many women tell us that their husbands proposed after they *moved away from, not toward,* the relationship. One woman booked a trip to Club Med with a girlfriend after dating her boyfriend for a year, another started getting very busy and unavailable on weekends, and a third talked about taking a job in another city. Then, their husbands proposed.

Remember, men don't necessarily propose when

you're cuddled up on the couch watching a rented video, but do so when they're afraid of losing you. In *Love Story*—a movie you should study like the *Bible*— Oliver proposes to Jenny (a *Rules* girl, if there ever was one) after she says she's planning to take a scholarship in France and after suggesting that their opposite (rich/poor) backgrounds would not mix well. Jenny wasn't grateful or loving at that moment—she almost broke off their relationship. (You don't have to go that far!) But be a *little* distant and difficult. The unobtainable is always more exciting; men very often want something more just because they can't have it.

If you are following *The Rules* (particularly *Rule #13: Don't See Him More than Once or Twice a Week*), you can't possibly live with him, by design or by accident. Women who tell us that they moved in with a man accidentally, as a result of spending long weekends with him, obviously broke a few rules along the way. You stay over a lot and one thing leads to another. First you get a drawer, then a shelf, and then a closet of your own. Before you or he realize it, you're having your mail delivered to his apartment and your friends are leaving messages on his tape machine.

Needless to say, this should not be happening. If you are doing *The Rules*, you never need a closet full of clothes and accessories at his place. Don't leave your toothbrush or bathrobe there. He should be begging *you* to leave things in his apartment and going out of his way to make shelf space. This invasion of space should not come from you. You are independent, you are not a crasher, you are always ending the evening (or the morning) first. (Besides, the less he sees of some of your less glamorous habits, like the way you floss your teeth or the sound you make when you slurp your coffee, the better.)

Is there any reason to live with a man if you haven't set a wedding date? Yes, and that's when *he* wants to and you don't! He's crazy about you and you're not so sure about him. In this case, he's taking the risk, not you. Still, proceed with caution. Living with him may prevent you from dating others and meeting someone you're crazy about, so how smart is it?

Don't Date a Married Man

*D*ating married (or unavailable) men is not only an obvious waste of time, but also it's dishonest and stupid. So why do so many women do it? Some feel it's better than dating no one, some find the very wrongness and danger of it (the secret hotel rendezvous) fun and exciting, and some hang on to the hope that one day the men will leave their wives for them.

All these women suffer from low self-esteem, or why would they settle for so little? We are not big advocates of therapy, but we believe it would be worth $125 an hour to find out why you would do this to yourself.

When you date a married man, you basically spend your life waiting for him to get separated. The deadline keeps changing from Thanksgiving to

Christmas, then Easter, then Labor Day. You wait and you sit by the phone on the off chance that his wife took the kids to her parents' house and he can spend an hour or two with you. And you cry when he can't see you on Valentine's Day or on his wedding anniversary or his wife's birthday. You are always second. In the beginning, affairs are full of promise and great sex. By the end, you are always crying on the shoulders of girlfriends and wishing his wife would die.

You will not get much sympathy from us. Dating married men is dishonest and totally contrary to *The Rules*. We do not take what is not ours. We don't date married men because then we get a reputation for it and no one will trust us around their boyfriends or husbands.

If you have recently met a married man that you are mad about, then you must practice self-restraint. If he is everything you ever wanted in a husband, be friends with him and hope he gets divorced. Until then, you must say to yourself that a single man like him exists somewhere out there for you. Then you must get busy, go to a singles dance, answer a personal ad or put one in a magazine, ask your friends to fix you up with someone. Take action. Join a gym, a church, or synagogue, or do volunteer work at a hospital. Never sit around dreaming about him or you might end up acting on your thoughts.

Dating a married man is easy because you can fantasize about his future availability. But, at the risk of sounding preachy, it bears repeating that you won't be at peace if you date a married man. Even if he leaves his wife, how do you know he'll actually marry you?

You're a *Rules* girl! Your life is never on the edge because of a man. Either a man is available and in love with you or he's taken and you have nothing to do with him romantically. You are not desperately waiting in the wings for his situation to change. You are not someone who waits and hopes while he takes his wife and kids to Disney World. You have a life of your own.

Lest you think we are being naive, we know that extramarital affairs happen all the time and that married men do at times divorce their wives and marry the girl they've been seeing on the side. We know one such woman who waited five years for a man to break up with his wife. They are now very happily married. She was very lucky. Are you willing to take that chance?

Slowly Involve Him in Your Family and Other *Rules* for Women with Children

*I*f you are a divorced or single woman with children, you should follow all *The Rules*. In addition, be especially careful when dating not to go on about all the pain from your first marriage or talk too much about your children.

When you meet a man at a dance or social situation, it isn't really necessary to mention your children at all. Let him take your phone number, then wait until he calls for you to gently weave it into the conversation. Don't say in a serious tone, "I need to tell you something." Remember in *Rule #19: Don't Open Up Too Fast*, we advise you to tell him about yourself very informally. Just casually say, "Oh, that's my son playing the piano" or something like that.

If and when he does ask you out for Saturday night, don't say, "Nine on Saturday is great, but I'll have to call the baby-sitter." Don't fill him in on details of raising children or how your ex-husband was supposed to baby-sit and is just so unreliable! It isn't necessary for a man to know you haven't gotten your alimony payments for the last three months and Tommy really needs new sneakers. Simply say, "Saturday at nine is great." At this point he is interested in *you*, not your family or your problems.

Please do not take this advice the wrong way. We are not telling you to be ashamed of your past or your children. Just wait a while before involving him. On your first few dates, it would be wise to meet your date in the lobby of your building or a restaurant so you don't have to introduce him to your children. This is as much for your date's sake as your child's. Your child should not have to meet every Tom, Dick, and Harry you date, only the serious contenders. Let the man be the one to bring up meeting your children. Make him curious about seeing them. Meeting your children should be an honor, not a routine occurrence. Just the way you hold back on other things in the beginning of your relationship, this too should take time. Make him work (again? yes) for the privilege of meeting your loved ones.

On the other hand, don't use motherhood as an excuse not to get out there and mingle. Having a child often means being in situations with married people and you might feel like a fifth wheel among all the couples you meet at PTA meetings and Little League. But remember that there are plenty of single fathers out there who want to remarry. So go to PTA meetings with a smile on your face and wearing a nice outfit. Socialize wherever you go with your child. You never know.

Practice, Practice, Practice! (or, Getting Good at *The Rules*)

*H*ow does one get good at *The Rules*? Unfortunately, the same way one gets good at playing the piano or tennis or anything else. Practice, practice, and more practice!

Once you're truly convinced you need *The Rules*, you should read this book over and over again until you've practically memorized it, then practice the principles as much as possible. Don't expect to get them right the first time or every time. We didn't. We broke rules, got hurt, and then eventually got serious and did *The Rules* as they are written.

Don't be discouraged. Just keep practicing! Try *The Rules* on all men at all times. Don't even say hello first to your doorman or the butcher at the deli. Let them say hello to you first and then just smile. Don't ignore them or anyone else, just practice *responding* rather than starting any conversation. Then later, when a man says to you, "I can tell you were the prom queen," and you weren't even asked to go, you will instinctively smile and say nothing. If, however, you are so used to blabbering all the time, then you might start explaining that you were thirty pounds heavier in high school and never really went out. If he is planning to marry you, you will eventually tell him all about your unpopular days, and by that time it won't really matter. We find that most women regret spilling their innermost feelings and thoughts on the first few dates. There will be less to regret if you learn to be quiet and mysterious more often. Reread *Rules* #19 and #20.

When the urge to call him comes, call a friend, your mother, the weather channel, walk the dog, write a letter, answer a personal ad, anything, until the urge passes, and it will. Call a friend who recently broke *The Rules* to remember how painful it is to chase a man. If you must call a man, better that you call a friendly ex-boyfriend than the current man of your dreams. The old relationship is over and there's not much to lose, but your new flame may lose interest in you if you pursue him.

The good news, girls, is that the more you practice *The Rules*, the easier it gets. If it's painful, remember, none of us do them perfectly. But try to do the best you can. Ending a phone conversation after ten minutes seemed cruel and impossible for us in the beginning, but the more we used a timer and did it anyway, the more natural it became to say, "It's been nice talking to you, but I really have to run."

It's not necessary to have a high IQ to do *The Rules*, just a certain degree of determination. In fact, highly educated girls have the hardest time with *The Rules*. They tend to think all this is beneath them. They'll say, "I went to graduate school, I'm not playing these games" or "I'm in management. I believe in being up front with men about my needs, my opinions, and who I really am. I refuse to be demure and smile when I don't *feel* like it."

If you think you're too smart for *The Rules*, ask yourself, "Am I married?" If not, why not? Could it be that what you're doing isn't working? Think about it.

But even if you're not desperate to get married right away, you never know when you'll change your mind. We've all met women who are certain in their twenties that they don't want two kids and a house with a picket fence. They tell us that their career, friends, and assorted romantic relationships are fine with them. So they don't bother to play hard to get when they meet men. They treat men like women — as friends. Then one day they meet a handsome man with gorgeous eyes. Suddenly they not only want him but want to have his children. These women either don't know about *The Rules* or have never practiced them. This is why you should always do *The*

Rules. You never know when you'll want to get married.

Another reason to do *The Rules* is so that people—men, women, bosses, parents—treat us well. When we don't do *The Rules*, we inevitably get hurt. When we do *The Rules*, we find out who really loves us. The answer might be painful, but better to weed out the uninterested parties than to carry on unsatisfying relationships. For example, you ask a man out and he says no, or he says yes to be polite and never calls again. You're hurt. But had you not initiated the date, he would never have hurt you. You have no one to blame but yourself! Or let's say your neighbor only comes by to borrow milk or when he's bored. You wish he would invite you to dinner. He doesn't. So you suggest dinner. He makes excuses. You're hurt. Again, situations of our own making! If someone is not asking you out, then they don't want to be with you. Go about your business and trust you will meet other people who genuinely like you and want to be with you. You might feel lonely and hurt for a while, but better that than being rejected.

The Rules can be used in many life situations. For example, if you love your sister too much, but she doesn't act particularly warm or nurturing toward you, don't call her every day. Just return her calls. Stop trying to "work things out" or go over childhood feelings. Just get a life so that your relationship with her is not the main thing on your mind. Be busy and when she finally calls you, be friendly. No one likes talking to someone who is angry or depressed.

You may be thinking, "But without so-and-so, I wouldn't have a friend to go to singles dances with or a summer house to visit." We know how you feel, but maybe you're supposed to go to dances by yourself or you're supposed to let go of so-and-so to make room for better friends. Just do *The Rules*. Don't think about the short-term results. Trust that you will find other ways to fill the emptiness. Maybe you'll take up running and meet someone on the track. Looking back, whenever we did *The Rules* and lost a relationship, we got a better one.

You see, whenever you love someone more than that person loves you, you are in a position to get hurt. *The Rules* way of thinking and acting protects you from unnecessary pain. It's a law of the universe that the more you try to get the love and attention of someone who doesn't naturally want you, the more frustrated and unhappy you will be. When we do *The Rules*, we give up the struggle. We accept that some people don't want us and we go on to the next. We don't force people to love us.

We had to change our definition of gratifying relationships. A gratifying relationship is long lasting and mutual, not short term and hurtful!

When we do *The Rules* in life, whether or not we want to get married, we create boundaries with people. Some of us get so overly friendly with our secretary, baby-sitter, or cleaning lady that they take advantage of us and don't do their jobs. We should be friendly but always remain the boss. We say yes to last-minute dates or let men get off the phone first, and then we wonder why we feel so empty. At work, we try too hard to make our coworkers like us, but they sense our motives and find us annoying.

The Rules are even useful in the business world. If your boss ignores you or isn't particularly fond of you, don't try to ingratiate yourself by making unnecessary conversation, asking about his or her weekend, suggesting lunch or bringing in homemade cookies. If your boss doesn't take you out to lunch, he or she doesn't want to. If your desks are near each other, don't constantly stare at him or her to make eye contact. Keep your eyes glued to your computer screen or the papers on your desk.

Everyone hates a brownnoser, so be professional and businesslike. Just do your work quietly and efficiently. Don't tell him or her how hard you work; don't stay late at the office to impress people. Don't look haggard or disheveled from having come in to the office early or stayed late the night before. Coworkers and bosses are actually more impressed by well-rounded people who get their work done during business hours and have a healthy social life. Dress as if you have a date after work.

If you think of *The Rules* as a manual for life rather than simply as rules for getting married, you might do them more often. Then, when you meet the man of your dreams, you'll have had plenty of *Rules* practice.

Even if You're Engaged or Married, You Still Need *The Rules*

*I*deally, we do *The Rules* from the minute we meet a man until he says he loves us and proposes. But if you were not lucky enough to learn about *The Rules* before reading this book, we suggest you do the best you can right now. Better to do *The Rules* now than not at all.

However, if you did not know about *The Rules* until now, don't think you can totally erase the way you related to your fiancé or husband from the beginning of your courtship. For example, if you initiated the relationship, called him up, asked him out, and so on, in order to make the relationship work, he'll always expect such things from you. He didn't worry about getting you to marry him, he knew he had you, you told him so with

125

every word and gesture, so on some level he may take you for granted. And chances are you still make things happen by initiating sex and/or romantic dinners, asking him about his feelings for you, wishing he would spend less time in the office or with his friends and more time with you. You might even wonder from time to time if he's having an affair.

If you didn't do *The Rules* at the beginning of your relationship, your husband might ignore you, talk to you rudely, or treat you badly. You might wonder, "Is his behavior the result of bad upbringing or something in his past?" Maybe. But we believe it's because you didn't do *The Rules*. He never needed to treat you like his dream girl. The same man who would act indifferent or ignore a wife who pursued him wouldn't dream of it with the woman who did *The Rules*.

Abuse doesn't happen in a *Rules* relationship because when you play hard to get and he works like hell to get you, he thinks you're the most beautiful, wonderful woman in the world, even if you're not. He treats you like a precious jewel.

But don't despair. Start doing *The Rules* now as best you can and he may notice a difference in your behavior and want you more. Here are five suggestions:

1. Don't call him at work so often. When you do,

keep it brief and practical ("What time is the movie?"). Don't call saying, "I miss you. Let's make love tonight." He should be calling you to express those sentiments.

2. Don't initiate sex, even if you want it badly. Let him be the man, the aggressor in the bedroom. Biologically, the man must pursue the woman. If you bring up sex all the time, you will emasculate him. Act as if you're a *Rules* girl on a first date. Be coy. Flirt when he tries to kiss you or bite your neck. This will turn him into a tiger.

3. Dress better, a little sexier. No man likes coming home to a woman wearing sweatpants or a bathrobe all the time. Try wearing tight jeans, a miniskirt, or a deep V-necked shirt in a bright color. Put on some makeup and perfume. Wash your hair. Pretend you're dating him.

4. Act independent. Always be *coming* or *going*. Don't sit on the couch waiting for him to come home. Don't bore him with details about your day or your aches and pains. Make lots of plans with friends, your kids, the neighbors. Go to the movies, to the shopping mall. Just go. This will make him desperate to catch a minute of your time. He will want to corner you in the kitchen for a kiss if he senses you're not around much. He'll get mad if you're on the phone when he's home because he'll want you all to himself. This is how it is when you do *The Rules*. He'll feel as if he

can never get enough of you. He'll start calling you from work to suggest dinners alone or a weekend getaway. This is what you want. Men love independent women because they leave them alone. They love chasing women who are busy. It gives them a thrill, as big as a touchdown or a home run.

5. Take up a hobby. Most men are content to sit around in a recliner on a Sunday afternoon and drink beer and watch football. Some bring work home from the office and spend the entire afternoon on the computer. Women tend to feel empty when their boyfriends or husbands don't include them in their plans or pay attention to them. It's imperative that you don't nag him to give up his hobbies, friends, or work because you're bored. You'll get more attention from him if you get even busier than he is. Make play dates for the kids, go out for a run or take an aerobics class at a gym. That will not only keep you busy but also will get you in shape, making you all that more attractive to him. He may wonder if other men are looking at you in your Lycra. That will be good for the relationship. It will make him want to turn off the TV or computer and be alone with you. You might get involved in a charity, read a book, take up a sport. The key here is to keep yourself independent and busy. This way you're not hanging around

him complaining that he's not paying enough attention to you!

Unfortunately, doing *The Rules* sometimes means
acting single (even if you're married with children)
all over again. Just be grateful you're not!

Do *The Rules*, Even when Your Friends and Parents Think It's Nuts

*R*emember your reaction when you first heard about *The Rules* or read this book? No doubt you thought the idea was crazy, dishonest, or extreme. "Why can't love be more natural? Why can't I ask a man out? After all, we're approaching the 21st century." But because your way didn't work, you became open-minded rather quickly. Something deep down inside you said *The Rules* just might be the answer.

Well, don't be surprised if the people around you don't support your new philosophy. Don't be surprised if they think you're nuts or question every move you make or don't make. When a man you're dating calls and leaves a message with your mother, don't be surprised if she hovers over you like a bee nagging you to call him back right away. Rather than say, "I can't call him back. I'm doing *The Rules*," just say, "Okay, mom, later, after I wash my hair." Keep postponing any *Rule*-breaking activity.

Your mother may hassle you, but it's your girl-friends that will probably give you the hardest time, possibly because they're not doing *The Rules* themselves. Don't be surprised if they take your devotion to *The Rules* as antifeminist. They may say things like, "You know, marriage isn't the answer. No man is going to fix you. There has to be a 'me' before a 'we.' You don't need *The Rules*. You need some good analysis to find out why you want to get married so much!" Don't say, "If I don't get married I'm going to kill myself" or "In Noah's ark, they went in twos." Just smile and change the subject.

Your friends might tell you that *The Rules* are dishonest, that you should let a man know exactly who you are, that it's rude not to call him or call him back. Unless they want to do *The Rules* themselves, don't argue with them or explain what you are doing. Just do *The Rules* quietly and let the results speak for themselves. The fact is that your friends and others might not have that burning desire to get married and have babies. They may be perfectly content in their careers and hobbies. You, on the other hand, can't imagine life without a husband. Neither could we. That's why we did *The Rules*—to ensure that the right man didn't get away.

We suggest you find like-minded women who believe in *The Rules*, want to get married, and support each other much like any support group. Call *them* when you want to call him. Don't bother asking your male friends if they like being pursued by women. They might say one thing and believe another. They will probably tell you that they're flattered to be called and asked out by women. What they won't say is that these are not the women they end up marrying or even dating.

Don't take a poll of men, or of married people for that matter. Your married friends or relatives might tell you, "I didn't do *The Rules* and I got married." They will poke holes into every rule, one telling you that she asked him out for the second date, and the other that she paid for the third dinner date. Don't argue with these people. Don't tell them you're doing *The Rules* because nothing else has worked. Just smile and say, "Oh, it's just for fun" and change the subject. Don't stop doing *The Rules* because married women tell you they didn't. How do you know what their marriage is like? How do you know that, because she pursued him, he isn't always neglecting her or spending too much time at the office? You want a *Rules* marriage, not just any marriage.

If you can't find any like-minded women to support you in doing *The Rules*, just read this book a lot, carry it around in your purse to refer to on long supermarket lines, and practice what you read as much as possible. Believe us, if you do *The Rules*, you'll be so busy dating your future husband to care or even think about what anyone else is doing or what anyone else thinks of what you are doing.

Be Smart and Other *Rules* for Dating in High School

*R*emember Janis Ian's song, "I learned the rules at seventeen, that love was meant for beauty queens?" The fact is, unless you look like Brooke Shields, high school can be very rough. There's acne and not fitting into the "in" crowd, not to mention having to go to the prom with a group because you don't have a date. Our *Rules* for high school won't guarantee you a date for the prom, but they will bring out the very best in you and make you more attractive to the opposite sex.

1. If you have really bad acne, go to a dermatologist. Cut out the greasy foods—pizza, potato chips, french fries—that make your face oily. Eat fruits and vegetables and drink six to eight

glasses of water a day. It also goes without saying that you should never spend Saturday nights lying on your bed. Have fun, make plans. Start believing now that you are a creature unlike any other! (See *Rule #1*.)

2. Spend your baby-sitting money on manicures and some pretty clothes. Wear makeup, but not too much. The idea is to look pretty, not overdone.

3. If you have a crush on a boy, your older brother's friend perhaps, don't act like one of the boys with him. Don't wear a baseball cap and sit around watching a ball game with the group. If he happens to be around, don't talk to him first. Be reserved and slightly mysterious. Let *him* notice you.

4. Always be out, mingling, not indoors, worrying. Go out to the beach, to the movies, to parties, not in your room dwelling on your flaws or quoting Sylvia Plath. When you go to parties, dances, or the beach, don't look wildly around for a boy to talk to you or ask you to dance. Don't chew gum and cackle. Walk erect as if you were balancing a book on your head, look directly in front of you, and seem self-contained even if you're lonely and bored to death.

5. If you have decided to have sex, wait until you are in a steady relationship. Use birth control, specifically a condom. You don't want to end up with an unwanted pregnancy or disease. Impul-

sive and irresponsible behaviors are not *The Rules*. In the '90s, it can be even cooler and safer to simply wait until you're more mature.

6. Don't smoke, take drugs, or drink alcohol, even if a very cool and good-looking boy is pressuring you to do so. Cigarettes are unhealthy, drugs and alcohol are mind altering and addictive and might make you do something that you don't want to do (like sleep with him on the first date). To do *The Rules* you must always be one step ahead. Drugs and alcohol make you messy and stupid—definitely not *Rules* behavior.

7. High school is a good time to take up sports like jogging, aerobics, swimming, or tennis. This is not only good for your body, but also for your social life. Lots of socializing goes on at running tracks and tennis courts. A healthy hobby will give you something to do in the summer. If you have the money, you might think about going to tennis camp where you can meet athletic boys your age. If you spend the summer working, on your days off make sure you go to the beach, get a (safe) tan, wear short shorts and bikinis, and go swimming, play tennis, or go Rollerblading.

8. *Act* confident even if you don't *feel* it. Notice what kinds of clothes, shoes, bags, jewelry, and hairstyles the most popular kids in high school are wearing. Don't try to be too different or frugal in this area. You'll feel lousy, so it's not worth it. To see what's hot and not, subscribe to *Seventeen* and

Glamour. Don't let your mind tell you that all of this is superficial and beneath you. (Save your mind for final exams and the SATs.) Don't you like boys who wear Polo shirts and cowboy boots when that's in fashion? Well, they like girls who wear what's on MTV and in *Seventeen.*

9. If the boy you like doesn't ask you to the prom, don't ask him. Better that you go with someone else who asks you or with a group. Start being a *Rules* girl now!

10. If you are lucky enough to have a boyfriend during high school, let *him* be the one to worry about the future. Choose a college that's good for you, not necessarily the one he is going to. (Who knows? You could follow him all the way to college only to have him dump you for a prettier girl in his dorm.) Go to whatever college you like and if he wants to see you, let him travel to *your* campus. Let him call and write you. Unless you're engaged, date others. Don't spend every weekend with your high school boyfriend, as some girls do who have a hard time separating. If you're meant to marry your high school sweetheart, it will happen despite the distance between you and despite any other men you meet in college.

Rule #29

Take Care of Yourself and Other *Rules* for Dating in College

*I*f you're going to college soon, we'd like to save you about four years of heartache. Here are seven mistakes not to make, now that *The Rules* are part of your curriculum.

1. Don't look up his class schedule and follow him around campus hoping he will eventually notice you. It's great exercise; otherwise, don't bother. Either he noticed *you* or he didn't.

2. Don't hang out in the dining hall for all three dinner shifts hoping to spot him at some point between 4:30 P.M. and 8:00 P.M., and end up gaining the "freshman twenty-five pounds" instead. (Do you really want to spend your college career in the cafeteria wondering, "When will so-and-so walk in?")

3. Don't have your girlfriend talk to his best friend and find out how he feels about you or if he even knows who you are, and/or become best friends with his fraternity or the girl on his floor, or do favors for anyone he knows. (Don't waste your time. No one, not even his best friend, can make him like you.)

4. Don't find out what his favorite albums or CDs are and play them all the time and don't wear, say, a Grateful Dead T-shirt if that's his favorite rock group. (Strange how women think that men are attracted to women who dress like men—sporty and even grungy. Yet, it's always the girls with cute jeans and fashionable shirts that get the guys.) *The Rule* is don't wear clothes to copy men, but to attract them.

5. Don't become a cheerleader or sports fanatic simply because he's on the football team. The same goes for taking up smoking or drinking because he does those things. Many women we know sipped Perrier on dates with men who drank alcohol and smoked and are now married to them. When it comes to habits, be yourself.

6. Don't offer to help him with Shakespeare if literature is not his strong suit or type his papers, hoping he'll date you. He either wants to or doesn't.

7. Don't be stupid about safety! Date rape has become quite rampant in college these days. Be wary. Study in a lounge or library rather than alone with him in his dorm room or off-campus

apartment. *Always* tell someone your whereabouts so they can keep track of you. *Rules* girls don't take chances. Don't take date rape lightly!

Now that you know what *not* to do, what *should* you do to attract your man on campus?

1. Study! After all, that's what you're there for! Smart is sexy!
2. Eat sensibly, even when your friends are gorging on unlimited cafeteria food and having pizza delivered to their rooms at midnight. We suggest you take fruit from the dining hall to save as a midnight snack. Tell yourself during the pizza party that your jeans will fit tomorrow. Remember, overweight is *not The Rules*.
3. Wear makeup. Read *Glamour* and other popular fashion magazines.
4. Get involved in some extracurricular activity, preferably one that you're interested in and where you can meet men naturally.
5. Don't sit in your room alone on Friday and Saturday nights reading Jean-Paul Sartre. Friday and Saturday nights are for mingling. You can read Sartre on Monday.
6. Pick a major and a career goal. College is not about picking up your MRS degree, although you may very well meet your future husband on campus. Still, you must exercise your brain, both for his sake and yours. Don't be a ditz!

Next! and Other *Rules* for Dealing with Rejection

*L*ife is not always fair. Fortunately, *The Rules* will help ensure that you are never unnecessarily hurt by a man. By behaving around men in a *Rules* way—independent and busy, not needy or aggressive—we do not put ourselves in a position to be hurt.

However, we cannot make a certain man like us or prevent a man from meeting someone else he likes better and consequently dropping us. And we can't stop an ex-girlfriend from winning him back. So what do we do when we get dumped?

Our natural reaction may be to stagnate and isolate, wish we were dead, not wash our hair or wear makeup, cry, sleep a lot, play sad love songs, and swear we'll never meet anyone as perfect as him again. We might find consolation in the refrigerator or talk nonstop about him to our friends. Obviously, this is ridiculous. Allow yourself about two days of such behavior, and then go on.

The Rules recipe for rejection is to wear a great dress and flattering makeup and go to the *very* next party or singles dance and tell your friends you're available for blind dates. Hopefully, you've been diligent about *The Rules* up to the breakup, and your social calendar is already full of dates. Remember, until the ring is on your finger or you're exclusive—by exclusive, we mean he's serious about marrying you and it's just a matter of time before he pops the question, as opposed to he's dating you until someone better comes along—you should be dating others. Nothing is better for cushioning the blow than the adoring attention of other men.

Whatever you do, don't lose your cool over this man. Now is the time to acquire faith, to believe in abundance. Tell yourself he is not the last man on earth, there are many others and certainly at least one out there for you. Talk to women friends who were dumped and then met "The One." They will tell you how happy they are now that so-and-so broke up with them, even though they didn't realize it at the time. Comfort yourself with uplifting slogans like, "When one door closes, another one opens" and any other positive philosophies you can think of.

Remember, *Rules* girls don't get hung up on men who reject them. They say, "His loss" or "Next!" They carry on. They don't tear themselves apart and wish they had done this differently or said this and not that. They don't write men letters offering to change or make things work out. They don't call them or send messages via friends. They accept it's over and get on with it. They don't waste time.

Don't Discuss *The Rules* with Your Therapist

*Y*ou're used to telling your therapist everything, so it's only natural that you want to tell him or her about *The Rules*. We strongly suggest you don't go into great detail for the following reasons:

1. Some therapists will think that *The Rules* are dishonest and manipulative. They will encourage you to be open and vulnerable in your relationships with men, to talk things out, not to keep your feelings of love or hurt inside. That, of course, is the basis of the therapeutic process. It's great advice for resolving issues with family and friends, but it doesn't work in the initial stages of dating. Unfortunately, you have to be mysterious in the beginning of a romantic relationship, not an open book.

2. Some therapists don't realize women's capacity for forcing themselves on men who don't want them and/or trying to make relationships happen. If they only knew how we wandered around campus hoping to run into men. If they only knew about the love poetry we've sent men, the interests we've pretended to have in order to make men like us (of course that never works), and if only they knew the lengths we've gone to get friendly with men's parents so that they would make their sons propose. If any therapist knew all these things—perhaps we never told them the whole story—they too would encourage us to focus on ourselves and not force things to happen. A woman in love with a man who is not in love with *her* can be dangerous to herself and him. Her only hope is to do *The Rules*.

3. Another reason not to discuss this book with your therapist is that you don't want to debate the merits of doing or not doing *The Rules*, otherwise you might lose your resolve to do them. It's hard enough to do *The Rules* when you believe in them, it's even harder when you talk to people who are downright against them. You should also not read any books that go counter to this philosophy or preach another method, particularly books that encourage women to pursue men or express their inner child.

Self-improvement is great—we all can be better in many areas. But self-improvement still won't get you the relationship you want. You may feel "whole" and "ready" after years of inner work and wonder why you still haven't snagged Mr. Right. The reason is you're not doing *The Rules!* Simply being a better person won't get you the man of your dreams. You have to do *The Rules!*

We suggest you try *The Rules* for six months before doing anything else. You can't do *The Rules* and something else at the same time. It just doesn't work!

If there's anything your therapist should be helping you with regarding *The Rules*, it's helping you develop the discipline and self-control necessary to do them!

Rule #32

Don't Break *The Rules*

*I*f you break *The Rules*, will he still marry you?

Women are always asking us this question. They do *The Rules* for a month or two and then stop. He still hasn't said "I love you," much less proposed; yet, these women are now asking him out, bringing up marriage, and in some cases cleaning and decorating his apartment. They don't realize that *The Rules* way is not a hobby, but a religion. We keep doing *The Rules* until the ring is on our finger!

Let's take the case of our good friend, Candy. We told her about *The Rules* and she admitted she pursued men and they never proposed. She finally became willing to do everything we suggested for the first month or so of dating a hard catch named Barry. *The Rules* worked so well for Candy that after two months Barry took her to Jamaica for a week. That's when Candy went back to her old ways, ignoring our suggestions. She didn't think she had to do them anymore!

During their vacation, Candy asked for assurances about their future and acted more amorously than he did by leaving love poetry on his pillow and initiating sex. When they returned to New York and continued dating, she suggested they get together during the week as well as on weekends. Whenever he kissed her good night, she suggested they have sex or rent a movie or do some other thing to prolong their time together. He finally told her, "I love you, but I'm not *in* love with you. It's really strange because in the beginning there was something about you I had to get to know, but then it changed for me." Sure, all that love poetry!

Candy had the strength to end the relationship shortly after he told her he didn't love her and didn't want to marry her. Men don't lie! When they say they are not in love, they mean it. They are giving you a hint to break it off and look elsewhere, which most women don't heed. More often than not a woman will stay put, wasting precious time and hoping against hope that a man will change his mind. Have you ever gone through this? Aren't you tired of the pain? After Candy and Barry finally broke up, she *never* broke *The Rules* again. We are happy to report that she recently got married by doing *The Rules* as they are written, which should give all women hope, as many women break *The Rules* before they finally do them!

Rules girls don't hang around where they are not wanted. They don't try to revive a love gone sour. If you've broken *The Rules* to the point where he's convinced he's out of love with you, don't stick around hoping for a second chance. Remember, sometimes distance and time can make a man realize he's made the biggest mistake of his life. He can always call you—he has your phone number! Your part is to move on. Better that you do *The Rules* perfectly in your next relationship than to hang around, tolerating the loveless feelings of your current flame. So the answer to the question, "Will he still marry me if I break *The Rules?*" is, sorry to say, "Maybe yes, but most likely, no." So why take a chance?

That's why we strongly suggest that you don't break *The Rules* at all. Of course, you might make mistakes as you practice them. If you have chased men your whole life, you can consider it progress if you stop writing men love letters but call them once in a while. However, we believe in striving for perfection. When you do *The Rules* perfectly, you don't have to worry about second chances because he won't fall out of love with you. When you break *The Rules*, you automatically take away the pleasure men get from pursuing you, and they end up resenting you for it. Then they treat you badly and you're left wondering if it was something you said, did, didn't say, or didn't do that caused the problem. The answer is simple: you broke *The Rules*.

Prepare yourself for the fact that you will usually want to break *The Rules* after you have been dating someone for a couple of months. You may feel that the relationship is slowing down or going nowhere. He starts calling less often or still hasn't brought up marriage. Your girlfriends are planning the wedding and you still haven't met his parents. You feel anxious. Naturally, you want to shake things up or move things along. You are tempted to send him heavy-handed greeting cards from the "relationship" section of the card store or a love letter telling him how much you care about him to bring him closer to you. Without his permission, you want to throw out his old leather jacket and buy him a new one. You act as if you are his wife and feel entitled—after all, he sees you every weekend and bought you flowers twice. You may even decide to try to patch things up between him and his dad, who haven't spoken for a while. Let's face it, you are out of control!

Persist in this kind of behavior only if you want to destroy any chance of his proposing! *The Rules* action to take when things slow down is more of the same: reread how to behave on the first few dates (see *Rules* #9 and #10). Just *hang out*, trust in the process, be patient, don't nag him, and don't make anything happen. If you still feel frustrated after a few weeks, then get moving yourself! Rent that summer share with your girlfriend rather than waiting for him to suggest plans, or sign up for tennis lessons with that new instructor at your health club. Don't hone in on the man you are dating—he will feel smothered, not loved. Move away, get busy and elusive, and he will either miss you or not. Best to find out now rather than later if he can live without you.

There are many ways to break *The Rules* in the early stages of a relationship. Here's another example:

After dating Ken for a month, Nicole decided to discard *The Rules*, which she had followed faithfully on the first four dates, and do what she *felt* like doing. If Ken was going to be her husband and father her children one day, she reasoned, why shouldn't she show him her true self? (Have you ever thought like Nicole?) So, for his birthday, she planned a big surprise party, partly as a ploy to meet his family and friends.

Not a weekend went by that Nicole's feelings didn't get the best of her. Once when they passed a playground, she suggested that they ride on the seesaw and swing on the swings, hoping to make him think about children. Ken found her behavior obvious and boring. The relationship went downhill from there. Nicole suggested couples therapy. He decided to break up with her and find someone else to date.

The lesson here is simple: don't break *The Rules*.

Don't make him a birthday party or give him an expensive gift, don't mention children, don't patch things up with his family, don't ask him out, and try not to call him very often. Basically, don't push yourself into his life or you won't be his wife!

When we pursue a man, a bell goes off in his head. *The challenge is over,* and his feelings start to fade. Suddenly, the romance turns to mud. Whatever he found adorable about you, he finds annoying. You're no longer his dream girl. It's as if you picked up the check or opened the door for him. You've taken his job away, you've done him a disservice.

So when you think that not calling him and other *Rules* are rude and hurtful, remember you are in fact helping him want you more. *The Rules* are actually *good* for him. So don't go by your feelings, just do *The Rules*.

The good news is that when a man is in love with you, he is not afraid to make a fool of himself by calling you five times in one day to tell you little, stupid things. (Yes, *he* can call you five times a day, but you can't or he'll think you're crazy!) *You* don't need to call him five times a day because when you do *The Rules* you have peace of mind. You don't need to call him for reassurance about the relationship because you're secure. And you

152

don't have to stay up until 2 A.M. making excuses about why he hasn't called in two weeks because when you do *The Rules* he calls every week, sometimes every day!

Rules girls don't fret too much. They do *The Rules* and, in return, men give them that secure, snug feeling of being loved and being asked out for Saturday night early in the week or, better yet, at the end of their last date.

Now we all know women who broke *The Rules* and got married anyway. We know one *Rule* breaker who is always initiating intimacy with her husband. He says he loves her, but he never pinches her bottom in the kitchen and would rather watch the 11 o'clock news alone in his reclining chair than cuddle in bed with his wife.

So if you break *The Rules*, at least muster the courage to end the relationship when he says he is not in love and it's over. It will save you a lot of time. It's a spiritual axiom that when you feel someone slipping away, let the person go. Don't try to find out why he doesn't love you or what you could have done better. That's begging and, frankly, it's beneath a *Rules* girl to do. Be firm when it's over, knowing that you'll be able to break down and cry with your girlfriends later.

Even if you think you could have done *The Rules* better, don't blame yourself. Just love yourself and do them better the next time. Don't call him, don't

153

talk to his friends about it, don't try to be buddies. It's over. Next! The relationship was not meant to be. There is somebody better out there for you. In the meantime, lining up a few dates is the best thing to do (and the best revenge).

Do *The Rules* and You'll Live Happily Ever After!

What can you expect to get when you do *The Rules*? The answer is total adoration from the man of your dreams. Otherwise, why else would we do them?

Let's face it, many of the things we ask you to do or not do in this book are downright difficult. Not calling him, not being intimate too soon, not bringing up marriage or children, and ending the date first require a great deal of self-restraint, patience, and determination. Sometimes we thought we would simply *die* at the thought of holding off having sex. And the agony of not calling him! There were many days when we just had to hear his voice.

So what kept us going? What made us continue doing *The Rules*? The incredible, unbelievable payoffs, twenty of which are listed below. So when you find yourself resisting doing a certain *Rule* (maybe you don't want to end the phone call after five or ten minutes because you're afraid he'll think you're rude and never call again), read this list and summon the courage. Remember, men want you more when you do *The Rules* and lose interest quicker when you don't!

1. The biggest payoff first: he wants to marry you! Most women bring up marriage or the future after a couple of weeks or months of dating a man. They want to know where the relationship is going. Most likely, it's going nowhere because men don't want to be pushed into proposing. As a *Rules* girl, you've been trained not to bring up marriage or kids. You talk about books, business, politics, football, and the weather. When you do *The Rules*, he ends up proposing.

2. When you are seated at a booth in a restaurant, he slides over and sits next to you. Sitting opposite you is just *too far away* when he's truly in love.

3. He sends you roses after you have sex.

4. He writes love notes or poetry for you and tapes them on the refrigerator door.

5. He finds your idiosyncrasies harmless rather than annoying. You never have to worry that he'll leave you if you don't change a bad habit.

He doesn't like it—but he doesn't leave you because of it.

6. He calls to see how your doctor's visit went.

7. He gives you little presents, jewelry, and flowers
on every possible occasion.

8. He gets angry when you don't pay attention to
him. He wants your constant attention and companionship. He doesn't ignore you. He's always
walking into whatever room you're in. You are
never a "football widow." He wants to take you
to the football game (even if you don't like the
sport or understand it) in order to spend more
time with you. He wants to do everything with
you!

9. He is always ready to make up after a fight.

10. He gets involved in every aspect of your life. You
don't bore him.

11. If you call him at work, he'll always want to talk
to you even if he is busy. He calls you from work
a lot anyway.

12. He doesn't like to work late because he wants to
see more of you.

13. When you have a cold or become ill, he still
wants to be with you.

14. He always wants the phone number of where
you are so he can get in touch with you.

15. He watches out for you.

16. He doesn't like it when you go to bachelorette
parties.

17. He *listens* when you talk to him.

18. When you walk around the house with very little on, he whistles, as though you were a babe on the beach.

19. Your picture is on his desk in the office and in his wallet. He always wants to look at you.

20. When he loves you, he loves your kids.

Hopefully, some or all of the above promises will motivate you to do *The Rules*. Still another incentive for doing *The Rules* is what you *won't* get:

1. No messy divorce. Instead, you have one of those made-in-heaven marriages. He'll take care of you when you're old. He really, really loves you. A *Rules* marriage is forever.

2. No outside counseling. He has no interest in couples therapy. When you do *The Rules*, he doesn't have big issues with you. He doesn't wish you were this, that, or different. His love for you is unconditional. Sure, he might wish you balanced your checkbook, lost ten pounds, or cleaned the house more often, but he is not seriously annoyed or upset about it. He finds it all amusing. Ultimately, he finds most things about you adorable. He doesn't feel the need to consult a professional to talk about his feelings. He's busy planning your next vacation or chasing you around the house for a quick kiss.

3. No anxiety. You're not walking on eggshells. You're not always wondering if you hurt his feelings or said the wrong thing. You know that he will always forgive you, not hurt you, that he is ready to make up with you at a moment's notice.

4. No physical abuse. When you do *The Rules*, he treats you like a fragile, delicate flower. He cups your face, rubs your back when you've had a hard day, and strokes your hair as if it were silk. You don't have to worry about being battered.

5. No cheating. When you do *The Rules*, he thinks you're more beautiful than other women (even if you're not). He doesn't want to have sex with anyone but you; he can't get enough of you and even wants to build up his biceps for you. You can leave him in a room full of gorgeous women and not worry. When he loves you, he loves you!

_____

Love Only Those
Who Love You

One of the greatest payoffs of doing *The Rules* is that you grow to love only those who love you. If you have been following the suggestions in this book, you have learned to take care of yourself. You're eating well and working out. You're busy with interests and hobbies and dating, and you're not calling or chasing men. You have high self-esteem because you are not sleeping around or having affairs with married men. You love with your head, not just your heart. You are honest; you have boundaries, values, and ethics. You are special, a creature unlike any other. Any man would be lucky to have you!

Because you love yourself, you are no longer interested in men who ignore you, cheat on you, hurt you either physically or emotionally, and, of course, any man who can live without you. The kind of men who once nauseated you because they were open books, called too much, wrote mushy cards, and told their friends and parents about you long before you said anything to your friends and parents, you now find attractive and desirable. Of course, we don't mean to suggest that you love someone simply because he loves you. No, you love whom you love. But when a man you are interested in is crazy about you, you are happy about it. You are not bored or turned off. You don't think, "Gee, this is too easy." *Love should be easy!*

As a result of doing *The Rules*, you have a new attitude. You love being loved. You think that anyone who thinks you're great is great, not a jerk. You have no desire to chase someone who hasn't noticed you, sought you out, or dialed your number and asked you out. Love is finally simple and sweet, not heart-wrenching and hard.

You might be saying to yourself, "But of course!" Yet, you'd be surprised how many of us only went after men who didn't want us. We thought it was our mission in life to reform men, make men who preferred blondes (if we are brunette) interested in us. We thought we had to *work* at making men love us. If love came easily, we were bored. Now we like love to be easy. We go to a dance or a party and we don't have to work at all. We just show up, do *The Rules*, and whoever likes us, likes us and who doesn't, doesn't. We accept whatever happens. We're laid back and confident. We don't struggle.

You're living painfree. No more lonely Saturday nights, no more waiting for the phone to ring, no more fantasizing about the man who got away or wanted your best friend, no more jealous tantrums, no more checking his desk drawers or coat pockets for incriminating evidence. To be adored and secure at last! That's the incredible payoff you get when you do *The Rules*, and you're going to love it!

Rule #35 _____

Be Easy to Live With

The Rules are about playing hard to get. Once you've got him, it's about being easy to be with.

Many things can go wrong in the first few months or year of marriage. You might have fights about where you'll live. There may be money problems or family problems. You thought you wouldn't have to work so hard, that you could work part-time and start planning for kids. He says he wants you to work full-time and have kids later. He thought you would make him home-cooked meals like his mother made his father and gets angry every time you open a can of tuna.

There may be more serious problems—for example, loss of job or illness. What is *The Rule* now?

The Rule is that as hard as you worked to play hard

to get is how hard you must work to be easygoing! Be kind, considerate, and patient; try to overlook his faults and build up his ego—tell him how good *he* looks, try to see things his way. Don't expect him to see things *your* way all the time.

It's natural to want to fly off the handle every time something goes wrong in the love kingdom—we all have fantasies of marital bliss. But you must try to be serene and unselfish, or you won't be a happy princess.

Let's say you've cooked him his favorite dinner, but he calls at the last minute to say he's working late and that you should eat without him. You're mad and want to scream into the phone, "But I cooked a special meal just for you!" Instead, take a deep breath and say something sweet like, "You've really been working hard lately. I'm so proud of you." Promise him a back rub when he gets home. Then get busy—read a book or clean the house. Don't tell him how disappointed you are and turn into a nag. Remember, he's working long hours for the both of you!

Or let's say it's your birthday and you know he's getting you something special but you have this thing about getting a dozen roses. So, you're on edge all day and wondering if you should give him a hint. You're also mad that you even have to say something!

So what do you do? Tell a friend, buy *yourself* flowers, and forget about it. Practice being happy with what you get instead of expecting him to fulfill your every romantic fantasy. Also, give it time. The roses will come. Life is long.

In general, remember that he works hard all day — whether or not you think he does. Don't hit him with every crisis the minute he walks in the door. And remember, small acts of kindness make for a great marriage.

This isn't always easy. Sometimes you just don't feel like shaving your legs, cooking him a hot meal, or being so sweet, kind, and loving. Your PMS might be in high gear. How do you keep yourself going?

We think it helps to use any stress busters — yoga, meditation, aerobics, running, biking, tennis, a spa weekend, and so on — to reenergize your batteries. True, it takes a lot more work to be a *Rules* wife than an ordinary one, but it's so much more rewarding in the long run, don't you agree?

You might also try reading spiritual literature, seeing a therapist, or joining a support group if things get too much for you or you find yourself constantly bickering with him about little things. But whatever path you choose, remember to keep the focus on *yourself*. Don't go into therapy or exercise with the idea of changing your husband or prodding him to get healthy, too. Change *yourself*, and your reaction to what he is or isn't doing.

On any given day, try to remember that an attitude of gratitude can go a long way. On bad days, try to remember the reasons you married your husband. In the middle of a fight with your husband, stop and recall all those bad blind dates, the seemingly endless search for Mr. Right. That should help you not say anything too mean in the middle of a fight like, "I wish I had never met you!" or "I should have married someone else." Don't dredge up the past or be mean-spirited and say things like, "Remember the time you were late for my sister's wedding?" Tell yourself, "I found Mr. Right — how important is this?"

If you want a happy *Rules* marriage, may we suggest a few more rules?

1. Don't go through his clothes, pockets, and drawers looking for anything — lipstick stains, women's phone numbers, hotel receipts, and such. Remember, if you're in a *Rules* marriage, he's not cheating on you. Then go about your business — read a book, exercise. Don't you have a letter to send or a drawer to clean out?

2. Don't open his mail unless it is specifically addressed to both of you. It is natural to think that what's his is yours, but that's not for you to decide. If he doesn't specifically show you something, or include you in certain things, it's none of your business. Besides, the less nosy you are, the more he will want to tell you — eventually.

3. Try not to raise your voice or scream too much. For some of us, who are more emotional than others, this is not always easy to do. For example,

when he watches the ballgame on TV all afternoon instead of helping you clean the house, don't
zap the tube off in a moment of anger. Nicely tell
him you need his help. If he still insists on watching the game, leave him alone. Tell yourself, "No
big deal." This kind of thing is not that important.
To lose your cool every time you don't get your
way gets you nowhere.

4. Don't hold him back from doing something he really wants to do, such as a ski weekend with a
bunch of friends. He should always feel free. He
should not think of you as the kind of person who
wouldn't want him to be happy because it means
not being with you. If you feel you have to hold
him back from anything, there's a problem in the
relationship. Don't try to control him. Remember,
we don't make things happen or stop them from
happening! We're easy to be with, we go with the
flow.

5. Always try to show utter contentment with him,
yourself, the world. Be carefree. You'll get less
wrinkles and backaches; you'll feel less stress.
He'll want you more when you're the easygoing
girl he dated—a creature unlike any other. Reread
Rule #1.

6. If you're feeling weak about *The Rules* and start
acting like your old pain-in-the-neck self—angry,
needy, not so nice—reread *The Rules* from the beginning. It will inspire you to act like a creature
unlike any other, and will remind you of the bene-

fits of doing so. Namely, your husband will find you irresistible all over again!

7. Make time for a healthy love/sex life and spend quality time together. We know that after a hard day of work, food shopping, aerobics, and so on, that you may not want to have wild sex or go to the football game with him. When you were dating you did things because you wanted to please him so that he would propose. Now that you have him, you think you don't have to try that hard.

True, you never have to do *The Rules* quite as hard as you did in the first three months of the relationship. But that doesn't mean you can be selfish or inconsiderate or lazy. Remember that if you want a good marriage, *The Rules* never really end!

Last But Not Least —
12 Extra Hints

1. When he asks you out, silently count to five before saying yes. It will make him nervous and that's good!
2. Don't call him even when you feel mean about not calling him. If he loves you, he'll call anyway. When he asks you to call him, call him once. Do the absolute minimum!
3. When he asks you out for ice cream, a drink, or to a football game when you wish you were going out for a fancy dinner, say "Sure!" Remember, you're hard to get but easy to be with! You'll go to an expensive restaurant another time.
4. When walking down the street, drop *his* hand first, ever so slightly.

5. *The Rules* are written in stone, but how you do them will depend on your temperament. If you're an overly nice, gushy girl, do *The Rules* like boot camp. The stricter, the better, that is, never call him, or return his phone calls very infrequently.

   But if you're already cool or aloof by nature, be extra sweet when you do *The Rules*. Call him once for every five times he calls you. Be affectionate. As long as you're not asking him out or moving in or bringing up marriage, you can show him you like him a little more on each date.

6. If he's being a bad boy, taking you for granted, or you want to shake things up to make him propose faster, book a trip for a week. If things are going well but you still want to make him miss you, plan a weekend away with a girlfriend. Tell him a week before you go, in a very innocent, sweet voice, that you're going to Florida with your girlfriend to get a tan and relax. "Nothing serious, hon, just some R & R."

7. If you are unsure about him, double date with a *Rules*-minded friend. She will tell you whether he's planning to marry you or not.

8. Even men who are in love with you and want to marry you will occasionally say things to irk you or make you nervous, such as, "I'll take you there if we're still seeing each other next year . . . you know how relationships go." Don't get paranoid, just ignore him. Most girls would make a big fuss

about it and get mad. *Rules* girls stay calm when men tease them.

9. Don't let him know you're *afraid* to be alone, to be without a man. Women who let men know how much they *need* to be with someone invite bad behavior. Then he knows you'll put up with anything not to be alone.

10. Don't get angry if he's taking longer than you'd like to propose. Most women want to be proposed to *yesterday*. Whatever you do, don't blow up at him and press the issue. You've waited this long, hang in there. If you're doing *The Rules*, it will happen!

11. Don't get sloppy about your looks. Continue to exercise. Men don't leave women who put on twenty pounds after the wedding or the first baby, but if you want your fiancé or husband to keep drooling over you, keep fit.

12. Read the newspaper and books so you can talk to your life partner about things other than your work issues or dirty diapers. Men want wives who can fulfill them mentally as well as physically and emotionally.

The Rules-at-a-Glance

ABOUT THE AUTHORS

ELLEN FEIN graduated from New York University, is married with two children, and lives on Long Island.

SHERRIE SCHNEIDER, a magazine writer, is married and lives in New Jersey.

Now that you've read *The Rules*, seminars are available to help you do them. For more information, please fill out this form and mail it to:

The Rules
FDR Station
P.O. Box 6047
New York, NY 10150
or call
(212) 973-0751

Name:

Address:

Phone#:

Age:

Profession:

Questions/Comments: